CAREERS
IN LAW

GARY A. MUNNEKE

VGM Career Horizons
a division of *NTC/Contemporary Publishing Company*
Lincolnwood, Illinois USA

Cover Photo Credit: Alberto Bernabe-Riefkohl is a professor of law at The John Marshall Law School in Chicago, Illinois. He teaches media, law, torts, and legal ethics. Courtesy The John Marshall Law School.

Library of Congress Cataloging-in-Publication Data

Munneke, Gary A.
    Careers in law / Gary Munneke. — 2nd ed.
        p.   cm. — (VGM professional careers series)
    Includes bibliographical references.
    ISBN 0-8442-4509-7 (hardcover : alk. paper). — ISBN 0-8442-4510-0
(pbk. : alk. paper)
    1. Law—Vocational guidance—United States.   I. Title.
II. Series.
    KF297.M86   1997
    340'.02373—dc21   97-3848
                                                                             CIP

Published by VGM Career Horizons, a division of NTC/Contemporary Publishing Company
4255 West Touhy Avenue
Lincolnwood (Chicago), Illinois 60646-1975, U.S.A.
© 1997 by NTC/Contemporary Publishing Company. All rights reserved.
No part of this book may be reproduced, stored in a retrieval
system, or transmitted in any form or by any means,
electronic, mechanical, photocopying, recording or otherwise,
without the prior permission of the publisher.
Manufactured in the United States of America.

7 8 9 0 VP 9 8 7 6 5 4 3 2 1

CONTENTS

ACKNOWLEDGMENTS

The author wishes to thank the many colleagues over the years who have contributed to his understanding of the legal profession: W. Page Keeton, J. Harris Morgan, Cullen Smith, Ann Kendrick, Peter Kutulakis, Roy Mersky, J. Kirkland Grant, Marty Africa, Roberta Ramo, Richard Bolles, the late Bob McKay, Jay Carlisle, and others. No list would be complete but these people come to mind. A special thanks to Sharon Clayton Walla, the author's wife and a practicing lawyer, and to Rich, Shannon, Kelly, and Matt.

ABOUT THE AUTHOR

Gary A. Munneke is a Professor of Law at Pace University School of Law where he teaches Torts, Professional Responsibility, and Law Practice Management. A 1973 graduate of the University of Texas School of Law, Professor Munneke is a member of the Texas and Pennsylvania bars. He is an active member of the American Bar Association, serving as Vice Chair of the Law Practice Management Section and on the ABA Standing Committee on Publishing Oversight. Previously he served the ABA as Chair of the Standing Committee on Professional Utilization and Career Development. He is a member of the editorial boards of *Barrister* and *Legal Economics* magazines, and the Task Force on the Role of the Lawyer in the 1980s. Professor Munneke has engaged in career counseling for law students since 1973 and has served as Research Chair and President of the National Association for Law Placement. He conducts LawStart seminars for students entering law school and has spoken extensively on the topic of careers in law.

Professor Munneke's other books include: *The Lawyers Handbook,* ed. (ABA-ICLE, 1992); *The ABA Guide to Legal Marketing,* ed. (ABA, 1994); *Materials and Cases on Law Practice Management* (West, 1991); *The Legal Career Guide: From Law Student to Lawyer* (ABA, 1984, 1992); *Barron's Guide to Law Schools,* 12th ed. (Barron's, 1996); *How to Succeed in Law School* (Barron's, 1994); *National Association for Law Placement 1985 Employment Report and Salary Survey* (NALP, 1986); *Opportunities in Law Careers* (VGM Career Horizons, 1981, 1986, 1993); *Non-Legal Careers for Lawyers: In the Private Sector,* with William D. Henslee (ABA, 1984, 1993); *Your New Lawyer: The Legal Employer's Complete Guide to Recruitment, Management, and Development,* ed. (ABA, 1984); and *The Report of the Task Force on the Role of the Lawyer in the 1980s* (ABA, 1981).

INTRODUCTION

This book is about careers in law. The premise is that law is not *a career,* but *many careers,* defined by the substantive fields in which legal problems are adjudicated. The common thread is that the law anticipates an orderly process of dispute resolution regardless of the substantive area.

A second premise of this book is that people will not or cannot resolve their disputes peaceably among themselves. The problems are too intractable. Individuals have difficulty expressing the reasons supporting their positions. They lack the resources to challenge others who interfere with their rights, or to defend themselves when challenged. For this reason, a representative system, where trained individuals stand in for the actual disputants, is needed in order to achieve justice.

It would be naive to suggest that this system always works. While we all hope for a better world, we accept the reality that lawyers operate in a less than perfect one. For those who are willing to enter this imperfect environment, law offers an exciting challenge. For those who need straightforward answers, simple solutions, clear-cut victories, and ultimate closure, law may be a frustrating career.

If, as some reports suggest, many lawyers are dissatisfied with their careers, perhaps they did not get an accurate picture of what work in the legal profession entails before they went to law school. It may be that they could have learned that law is not for everyone before investing so much time, money, and ego. It may be that they could not recognize that there are many different ways to "practice" law, and that not all require the same type of person.

This is not the first book on careers in law. Some are unabashed boosterism; others try to warn you away. Some approach the topic from the perspective of "how to" (get into law school, succeed in law school, get a job); some focus on settings where lawyers work (law firms, corporations). Some are humorous; others are loaded with statistical information. All these titles have a place in the literature of the law, and many provide valuable insights and information on Careers in Law.

This book looks at Careers in Law in terms of what lawyers do, based upon substantive areas of practice. Since law is becoming increasingly diverse, it is increasingly difficult to make generalizations that apply to all lawyers. As practice segmentation and specialization increase, more and more lawyers define themselves substantively, just as doctors have for decades.

Part I of this book discusses the legal profession today. It looks at the nature of legal services, the delivery of legal services, and the distribution of legal services. It will help the reader to comprehend a larger picture within which various fields of law exist.

Part II presents overviews of several major practice areas. There are 18 chapters that each deal with a specific category of law. Also included is a chapter on "boutique" practice areas, clearly defined specialties less prevalent in the legal profession than the major practice areas.

Taken together, legal careers may be viewed as a complex matrix involving several variables: substantive field of law, type of organization, location of organization/services, critical skills and values, type of position (path) and type of services rendered. (See Chart 1.)

The decision to pursue a career in law involves finding a place within this matrix where individual skills, interests, values, and aspirations can thrive. The process of decision making is beyond the scope of this book, in part because career choices involve a lifelong process. Individuals make choices in high school, college, law school, and post-law school that determine where within the matrix they will move.

CHART 1
Legal Career Variables

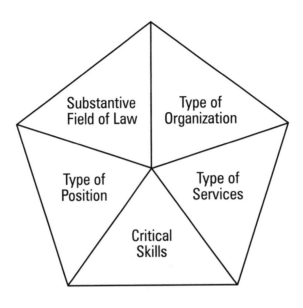

Part One
The Legal
Profession Today

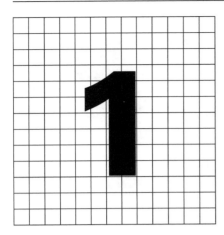

LAWYERS IN AMERICA

IMAGES OF LAWYERS

They called it the trial of the century: O.J. Simpson, the famous football and movie star, accused of brutally murdering his ex-wife Nicole Brown and her unfortunate friend Ron Goldman. From the first news of the killings until the final verdict was announced, virtually everyone in America was inundated on a daily basis with news of the proceedings. Cameras in the courtroom and commentators in the studio provided an unprecedented opportunity for people to see the legal system at work in all of its ponderous manifestations.

There have been many famous trials. Some you may be familiar with include: The Lindbergh kidnapping, the Rosenbergs who were accused of spying for the Russians during the cold war, Aaron Burr who killed Alexander Hamilton in a duel, and the Scopes Monkey Trial, which tested the right to teach evolution in the schools. In their day these cases captured the attention of the populace. The Simpson case was different: the electronic media, the personalities, the social issues all contributed to focusing the attention of the public on the proceedings. And what people saw was not always pretty.

Regardless of whether you think O.J. is guilty or not, and regardless of whether you thought the trial was a circus or drama, you had to admit that it was at times fascinating. Despite the drawn out procedural maneuvering and the tedious elicitation of factual testimony, there were moments when almost any observer could feel the excitement. If you didn't, you probably would have little interest in becoming a lawyer.

Law is an exciting profession and lawyers do work that makes a difference in people's lives. Ask O.J. Sometimes, however, highly publicized trials, which are most often criminal prosecutions, leave the impression that all of law is criminal practice, or that all lawyers are just like Johnnie Cochran, F. Lee Bailey, Marcia Clark, and Chris Darden. As this book will demonstrate, nothing could be further from the truth.

There are many things that people do not know about law and lawyers. Lawyers are often misunderstood. Laypeople ask, "How could you represent that criminal? How could you get him off on a technicality?" The lawyer's response may be that everyone deserves competent legal representation in the form of a lawyer who will require the state to prove its case, and that this basic dynamic is what holds the system together. Such an answer may be less than satisfying to a parent whose child has been raped and murdered, or a farmer whose land is foreclosed. The reality of law is that not all the parties to a dispute get what they want; in fact, a trial inevitably produces winners and losers. The antagonists themselves are seldom simplistically good or bad. They usually represent very different perspectives on what is right or wrong. If they had been able to resolve their differences amicably, lawyers wouldn't be involved.

HISTORICAL PERSPECTIVE

The American public maintains a love-hate relationship with the American legal profession. The legal profession has both attracted and repelled generations of Americans. Lawyers were praised as the drafters of the Declaration of Independence and the Constitution, but they were excluded from some of the earliest American colonies. Long before the Mayflower sailed to the new world, Sir Thomas More's *Utopia* declared, "They have no lawyers among them for they consider them as a sort of people whose profession is to disguise matters."

Even Shakespeare offered a number of unkind comments about lawyers. Ironically, Shakespeare's most famous lawyer line, "The first thing we do, let's kill all the lawyers," is actually an endorsement of the legal profession. The speaker, Jack Cates, was one of a cabal seeking to overthrow the legitimate throne of England. These rebels would replace a system of laws with a dictatorship based on personal power. To Shakespeare, the rebels were a threat to order and justice, while lawyers stood in the path of anarchy. In *The Merchant of Venice,* the lawyer Portia defends the merchant Antonio against Shylock the money lender, arguing that her client's bond of a pound of flesh could not be extracted without also sacrificing his blood, which was not a part of the bargain.

Accordingly, Shylock could have his pound of flesh only if he could take it without the loss of a single drop of Antonio's blood.

In this country, it is widely known that many of the fathers of the American Revolution were lawyers. De Toqueville proclaimed that lawyers became the new aristocracy after longstanding ties to the British monarchy were broken. But anti-lawyer sentiment, festering from the colonial period, reemerged as a part of Jacksonian democracy. In fact, lawyers were viewed with disfavor during much of the nineteenth century.

In those days, anyone who wanted to become a lawyer could do so by reading the law until he was prepared to sit for an oral examination by a qualified member of the bar. Upon successful completion of this examination, the new lawyer was permitted to pass the bar—quite literally to go on the other side of the rail separating the judge and lawyers from the courtroom gallery. The image of Abraham Lincoln, studying his law books by firelight, practicing law in rural Illinois, and eventually parlaying his skills of elocution into a political career captures the spirit of that era. Others lawyers of Lincoln's period served apprenticeships to practicing lawyers, but only a small percentage were formally educated in law schools (which resembled modern law schools very little). In contrast, today's law schools, an innovation of the 1870s, train virtually all new lawyers in the United States.

In addition to changes in legal education, other developments of the last quarter of the nineteenth century included the establishment of standardized bar examinations, the adoption of ethical codes, and the evolution of strong self-regulating bar associations. These changes helped to overcome negative reactions against a legal profession that often failed to maintain the image and character embodied in Honest Abe.

Although the pendulum may have swung several times in American history between pro- and anti-lawyer sentiment, the legal profession has always maintained an important position at the heart of the American psyche. A nation founded on legal principles has frequently turned to lawyers to help strike the balance of power between order and liberty, and between the individual and the state.

The process of forging workable solutions to difficult problems involving intersecting rights and duties is what law is all about. Law is an inescapable element in virtually every form of enterprise in the modern world. Lawyers and judges are charged with understanding, articulating, and interpreting the matrix of rules and procedures in an environment made more complex by the rich diversity of American society.

The alternative to the rule of law is not really different from what is was when Shakespeare wrote *Richard III*. Anarchy, dictatorship, and vigilante justice await at the fringes of the law, and stand ready to seize the reins of power when and if the rule of law breaks down.

A career in law by definition means a commitment to the peaceful resolution of disputes. Because disagreements are unlikely to be eradicated from our social, religious, political, moral, and economic landscape, the need for lawyers is not likely to disappear. In fact, as the world becomes more diverse, so do the settings in which law is practiced.

Lawyers have been involved in every step of the country's growth from colonial backwater to world superpower. Lawyers have served in all the branches of government; they predominate the judiciary where in all but a few courts judges must also be lawyers. Lay judges are found only in the lowest level courts, such as justice of the peace and traffic courts. Lawyers comprise a far greater proportion of the legislative branch than other professions and businesses. The executive branch of government at the federal, state, and local levels also includes a multitude of lawyers.

In the private sector, lawyers have contributed to society in countless ways outside of the private practice of law. They have gained recognition as leaders in industry, authors, reporters, artists, and inventors. Some lawyers, known for their contributions in others fields, are not widely recognized as lawyers. Many of them have ventured far from the traditional practice of law.

Although the majority of lawyers actually practice law, a great many (approximately 30 percent) do other things. Some of these are law-related (e.g., teaching law, serving as judges or arbitrators) but do not involve the representation of actual clients. For the record, lawyers who practice law within a corporation are considered practicing lawyers because the corporation itself is considered their client. Many other lawyers have left the legal profession altogether, and engage in activities that have little to do with the legal system.

Many lawyers are dissatisfied with their work as lawyers and substantial numbers of them defect from the practice of law for other careers each year. This is so for a number of reasons. First, practicing law is not for everyone, and some people do not discover this until they start to practice. How many of them would have made a different decision through better career planning is a matter of some debate. Second, the early years of practice are the worst. New lawyers must cope with the frustrations of inexperience on the job, work schedules very different from school, and changes in their personal lives. The cases they handle are frequently less interesting than those handled by more experienced lawyers. Third, the truth is that lawyers have always left the practice of law to do other things. Look at Lincoln. Many lawyers find that their work as practicing lawyers leads them to other fields of endeavor; for these lawyers, law is a bridge, not a dead-end street.

Lawyers in America are thriving whether or not they are part of the formal legal profession. As entrepreneurs, employees of businesses, artists, and philanthropists, they contribute to society. And most of them utilize their legal background on a regular basis. Certainly, there are dropouts; it would not be hard to find lawyers among the urban homeless. Such harsh realities are endemic to modern society. The tragedy of homelessness cuts across occupational lines. It should not be an indictment of the law that not everyone succeeds in the traditional forms of practice. The amazing facet of law is that it is so versatile that it opens doors and supports countless other career choices.

STATISTICS ON THE PROFESSION

There are approximately 900,000 lawyers in the United States today. Over 60 percent of them engage in the private practice of law, from individual practitioners to megafirms comprised of more than 1,000 lawyers. The lawyers include both owners of law firms (solo lawyers and law firm partners) and employees (associates and other non-owner classifications).

About 40,000 new lawyers are licensed to practice law every year. And despite anecdotal reports to the contrary, most of these new lawyers are assimilated into the legal profession, most as law firm associates, but many as in-house corporate counsel, government legal counsel, judicial law clerks, legal services lawyers, and a variety of other positions. (See Appendix B.) The range of salaries for recent graduates is between $15,000 and $85,000, with a median of $40,000.

Close to 90 percent of the lawyers in the United States practice in metropolitan areas, where population and business activities are centered. The number of small town lawyers has declined since 1950, resulting in an overabundance of lawyers in many cities and a shortage of lawyers in some rural areas.

Surprisingly, there is very little empirical research on lawyers and the legal profession. A variety of bar associations, professional organizations, and legal periodicals produce statistical reports, economic surveys, and other information on the practice of law. Those who are interested in law as a career may want to pursue some of these information sources as they evaluate the decision to pursue a career in law.

The overall picture to emerge from the various available sources is that of a large, powerful, and increasingly diverse legal profession. Whereas lawyers compete fiercely for an expanding base of potential clients, the number of people whose legal needs is not fully met has increased as well. While the percentage of lawyers practicing alone has decreased over the past half century, the actual number of solo practitioners has increased. This picture may seem contradictory, but it just may be difficult to make generalizations about such a large and diverse group.

MYTHS ABOUT LAWYERS

The following sections address some of the common myths about lawyers. They may have some roots in reality but generally they represent fantasy more than fact.

Lawyers Are Rich   Compared to the homeless or to single mothers on welfare, most lawyers are rich. Compared to Bill Gates, the founder of Microsoft, or Donald Trump, most lawyers have little real wealth. In other words, the word "rich" is relative. A newly graduated lawyer who goes to work for a Wall Street law firm may earn $85,000 during his or her first year of practice. That same graduate may have to pay off student loans of $50,000 to $100,000 or more, relocate and obtain housing, acquire a professional (as opposed to student) wardrobe, and undertake other expenses that were not incurred during school. Graduates who start out at less than the top salaries may have to struggle just to make ends meet.

Imagine two individuals who graduate from high school at the same time. Bob starts to work immediately after graduation as a laborer for $10.00 per hour or $20,000 per year. Judy goes to college and law school incurring debt at a rate of $20,000 per year for tuition, books, room, board, and other educational costs. Judy pays for her education with student loans. When Judy graduates from law school she will be $140,000 in debt, while Bob will have earned $140,000. If Judy goes to work for a law firm that pays her $40,000 per year (a median salary; only a few hundred of the nation's 40,000 law graduates in 1995 earned top salaries of $85,000 per year), she will be making $20,000 annually more than Bob (assuming, of course, that he has never received a raise). At this rate it will take fourteen years for Judy to pull ahead of Bob in terms of earned income. By that time, both will be around forty years old. Thereafter, the economic scale will tip in favor of Judy.

Sam, a college graduate who goes to work at $30,000 per year while Judy shells out $20,000 to go to law school, will reach a $150,000 differential by the time Judy graduates. Earning $10,000 per year more than Sam, Judy would surpass him in fifteen years (assuming that Sam and Judy borrowed the same $20,000 per year to go to college). The point of these illustrations is that the opportunity cost of a legal education is substantial. Additionally, if Bob and Sam receive ordinary raises, make sound investments or receive bonuses, overtime, or other benefits, Judy may take even longer to catch up.

A practicing lawyer named Sharon, who has her own firm, may spend 60 hours per week in her office. As a solo practitioner she can only devote about half her time to client matters (1,500 hours per year). If Sharon can bill her clients at an average rate of $100 per hour and collect all her accounts, she can bring in $150,000. But after she pays rent, secretarial salaries, and other office expenses, she may take home $75,000 or less. If Sharon wants to make more money next year she will have to work harder, charge more, or reduce her overhead. She will never get rich at this pace.

Some lawyers produce annual incomes in seven figures. Houston attorney Joe Jamail earned over $250,000,000 for representing the Pennzoil Corporation in a successful interference with contractual advantage suit against Texaco. The chances of any given lawyer winning such a case are less probable than winning the lottery.

The simple truth is that most lawyers earn a good living, but truly wealthy lawyers were born that way, married into money, went into business with their clients or others, or were lucky and skillful enough to win a big ticket lawsuit. This may come as a surprise to those who think that all lawyers are rich.

Lawyers Are Crooked

The stories of dishonest lawyers are legion. Most of those involved in the Watergate affair during the early 1970s were lawyers. A lawyer from New York, in 1991, disappeared with $20 million of his clients' money, which the lawyer was holding in escrow. Judges take bribes. Law firms overcharge their clients. One would think that dishonesty was a prerequisite to passing the bar.

A variation on the theme of the "shyster" lawyer is the wily advocate who, while doing nothing illegal, takes advantage of others including his clients. This enduring image hearkens to the story of a lawyer who meets two men in the road arguing over the ownership of an oyster. Volunteering to help settle the dispute, the lawyer swallows the meat, and gives each man half of the shell.

A third example is that of the ambulance chaser, the lawyer who will do anything to get a case. There are numerous media portrayals of sleazy lawyers taking advantage of people during a personal crisis or tragedy.

Periodically, some group will report that lawyers fall at the bottom of some poll of perceived integrity. And everyone it seems has at least one lawyer story: The Pope dies and goes to heaven where he is shown his new quarters, a modest bungalow in a quiet neighborhood. In the distance is a fabulous mansion with manicured lawn and ornate trim. "Who lives there?" inquires the Pope. "John Smith, a lawyer," replies St. Peter. Sensing that the Pope may be slightly miffed by this revelation, St. Peter adds, "We have lots of popes here, but we've never had a lawyer before."

The truth is that there are dishonest lawyers. Some members of the bar are predatory, avaricious, and amoral in their dealings with clients. Every month the pages of the bar journals contain the accounts of lawyers who have been reprimanded, suspended, or disbarred. Most often these lawyers are charged with neglecting their clients' cases, misusing clients' funds, or being convicted of some felony outside of the practice of law. Many more lawyers are privately reprimanded by attorney grievance committees.

To put information such as this into perspective, remember that there are around 850,000 lawyers in the United States. Reports from state bar disciplinary counsel indicate that only a minuscule number of lawyers are actually convicted of ethical violations. While it is disturbing that anyone in a position of trust would abuse that trust, the percentage of lawyers who fail to adhere to the ethical standards of the profession is small.

The various jurisdictions try to prevent such events from occurring. Applicants for the bar undergo rigorous character and fitness reviews. Practicing lawyers are subject to discipline for failure to maintain professional standards. Some states require lawyers to complete an ethical component of mandatory continuing legal education. An increasing number of jurisdictions maintain client security funds to protect clients against larcenous lawyers. More enlightened bar associations, recognizing that breaches of trust often reflect some other personal problem such as alcohol or drug abuse, offer counseling and intervention for impaired attorneys.

In short, lawyers are not perfect, but the profession strives to maintain standards of integrity and honesty. Although an alarming number of lawyers do step out of line, the ranks of those who are honest and trustworthy are far more numerous. The number of lawyers who have dedicated substantial portions of their professional lives to public service is noteworthy, and exceeds many other professions.

Part of the reason that some people think lawyers are corrupt is that they do not understand the role of the lawyer. Lawyers are required to zealously represent their clients within the bounds of the law. This means that lawyers may need to call for an interpretation of contractual language not apparent on the face, or argue a highly technical point of law that would produce an unpopular result, but one favorable to the client. In perhaps the most conspicuous display of this role, criminal defense lawyers are required to give their clients the best possible defense, and to force the state to prove its case beyond a reasonable doubt. If lawyers try to bribe a juror, that is wrong. But if lawyers successfully suppress important evidence of the state because the police failed to obtain a proper search warrant, they are doing their job (and protecting the integrity of the system for all citizens).

Too Many Lawyers

The myth that there are too many lawyers has been popularized by the media, and promoted by numerous commentators both within and without the bar. As recently as August 1991, Vice President Dan Quayle alluded to the large numbers of lawyers in a speech to the American Bar Association calling for reform of the civil justice system.

Almost all "too many lawyer" attacks start with the proliferation of lawyers. Next, they point out that the growth of the legal profession has outpaced the economy as a whole, and that America has more lawyers than any country in history. Then, the argument branches into two seemingly contradictory limbs. One group, comprised mostly of lawyers, claim that there is not enough business for all these lawyers and that lawyers' incomes will fall, unsuccessful lawyers will be tempted to act unethically, and that professionalism will decline. They will point to clear evidence to support these contentions. The other group suggests that there are too many lawsuits. Citing a litigation explosion, they point to the large number of lawyers feeding the explosion and undermining less destructive and less expensive alternative methods of dispute resolution. Both groups blame "too many lawyers" for the evils they perceive.

Charges such as these go back decades if not centuries. *Law Office Management,* by Dwight McCarthy published in 1926 asserts "The conditions surrounding the practice of law are changing. Competition is becoming keener. The rapid increase in the number of lawyers tends to divide up the business. Banks, trust companies, and title companies are encroaching on the lawyer's presence . . . Moreover, the demands on the lawyer's time are multiplied while consultation and litigation fees are not commensurate with the increased standard of living . . . and routine office work encroaches on the valuable time that should be devoted to more important matters." Such sentiments could have been planned yesterday.

At the heart of Thomas More's utopian theories was a desire to reduce litigation as a form of dispute resolution. What critics of lawyers fail to appreciate is that lawyers can help resolve disputes in many settings other than litigation, such as negotiation, counseling, mediation, arbitration, and education. The number of disputes may be only marginally correlated to the number of lawsuits. Maybe critics are saying we Americans should get along better; that may be so, but until we do, we will need lawyers to help resolve our disputes. The alternative of a breakdown of law and order is unappealing to most.

A theme that has not been flaunted since the 1970s is that many Americans do not have adequate legal services. Many working class Americans cannot afford legal services and only turn to lawyers in a crisis (e.g., they are arrested for DWI). If such a situation exists, then the nation may need more, not fewer, lawyers. The problem is economic: how do we pay all these lawyers? If lawyers' incomes are, in fact, threatened already, where is the money to support more lawyers, even if the need is present?

A final factor in the debate about "too many lawyers" is the demographic distribution of lawyers. As lawyers have moved to urban areas and the Sun Belt, basically following the population, the supply of lawyers has impacted differentially on different parts of the country. In most cities the ratio of population to attorneys is 200:1 or less. In rural areas it often exceeds 1,000:1.

It may be a myth to state in the abstract that there are too many lawyers, but in practice, the truth of the statement depends on who you are and where you live. Those considering a career in law should think about this issue, and not accept the simplistic answer sometimes offered.

FUTURE OF THE LEGAL PROFESSION

The pace of change in twentieth century society has been remarkable, with innovations transforming life at an accelerating rate. Many authors in recent years have tried to analyze this change and interpret it. One of the best efforts was Alvin Toffler's *Future Shock,* which hypothesized that changes were occurring in the world faster than many people could process them. The response was a feeling of hopelessness. Toffler suggested that in order to cope with change, it was necessary to understand *the process of change* as well as specific changes taking place in society.

The legal profession has changed dramatically over the past few decades. Although the first half of the twentieth century brought the typewriter, the telephone, and other technological advances, these pale in the face of changes in the profession since 1960. The photocopy machine, dictation equipment, advances in telecommunications, and the microcomputer all have contributed to fundamental shifts in the way law is practiced. Likewise, CD-ROM, optical laser disk, and imaging technologies point to continued evolution in the practice of law.

Some of the trends resulting from developments in society and the profession include:

Automation—Lawyers are turning increasingly to technology to help them practice law. Computerized word processing, case management, document assembly, financial analysis, accounting, timekeeping, and billing systems are rapidly replacing manual methods in even the smallest firms. Computerized legal research, tapping vast data banks for information, is becoming a necessity rather than a luxury. Document retrieval in litigation has become automated. Some jurisdictions provide for electronic filing and serving of process. On-line editing of draft documents is common. In 1980, only the largest law firms could afford computers. Today, these machines are utilized by almost all lawyers.

Autonomy—Clients today are more sophisticated and cognizant of their rights. They are less willing to delegate to others major decisions about their lives. They demand more information in order to make informed decisions. Lawyers must meet their clients' expectations in order to provide quality legal services. If they fail to communicate with and to satisfy their clients, lawyers can expect to be sued themselves.

Business—Because of competition not only from within but also from outside the legal profession, lawyers have been forced to market their services. There is more of a free market now than prior to 1977 when lawyer advertising was upheld by the U.S. Supreme Court in *Bates v. State Bar of Arizona*. Those lawyers who can bring in the business (the "rainmakers") more often than not call the shots in their firms.

Restructuring—While many firms have grown dramatically during the last two decades, many others have split, downsized, collapsed, and reorganized during the same period. A large number of alternative organizational forms have emerged, such as limited liability companies, branch offices, group legal services offices, ad hoc law firms (that come together for just one case), and contract lawyers.

Globalization—From Eastern Europe to the Common Market to the Pacific Rim to Latin America to the Middle East to the Third World, global interdependency is growing. This trend means that lawyers of all kinds are more likely to handle problems with international implications than at any time in the past. Not the least of these international issues is the environment, where problems know no borders.

Diversity—The legal profession is growing more diverse in its makeup, reflecting changes in society at large. In the future, the growing needs of these ethnic communities will require increasing numbers of lawyers. Particularly in the West and Southwest where the Spanish language has created a bicultural environment, Spanish-speaking lawyers will be in great demand.

Specialization—More lawyers are choosing to concentrate their practices in one or a very small number of substantive fields. The risk of malpractice suits, the overwhelming demands of staying abreast of changes in the law, and the need to target marketing efforts to a narrow band of clients have all contributed to a decline in the number of generalists in law. Although not as common as in medicine, specialization is a growing phenomenon in the practice of law.

The legal profession today can expect to continue to evolve. Those entering the profession in the 1990s at the age of 25 should expect change to be the one constant over the next forty to fifty years of their careers. It may not be possible to foresee the future, but it is feasible to make educated guesses about where our world is going. We can be sure that whatever the future brings, people will have problems and disputes. As long as this central dynamic of human existence does not change, lawyers will have a role to play.

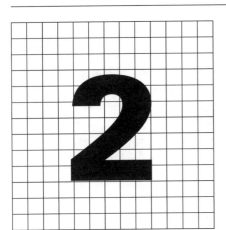

WHAT LAWYERS DO

In order to understand what lawyers do, it may be useful to look at what services they provide. Law is a personal services industry, meaning that the lawyer or law firm performs work at the direction of a client for the benefit of the client. The nature of the relationship is contractual. The client normally has some objective such as forming a corporation, filing a lawsuit, or getting a divorce.

The lawyer, however, is not like an employee who works at the direction of an employer. The lawyer is entrusted to make certain decisions about the conduct of the client's case. While the client controls the objectives of the representation, the lawyer is said to control the way the case is handled.

Because the lawyer possesses special skills, the relationship between lawyer and client is predicated on the lawyer's exercise of those skills with the same degree of reasonable care that a lawyer of ordinary prudence would use. A lawyer who does not act with such care can be held liable in a malpractice action by the client. Since clients today are more willing to sue their lawyers than in the past, lawyers must constantly strive to provide competent services.

This chapter is divided into two parts: the roles of lawyers and what lawyers do. The first part recognizes that lawyers may be called upon to serve in a number of distinct roles. Although we frequently think of lawyers primarily as advocates, they perform a number of other roles. The second section covers different types of work lawyers pursue. Note that a lawyer involved in a single type of work may perform several different roles. For instance, litigation may involve advocacy, negotiation, and advising.

THE ROLES OF LAWYERS

The American Bar Association *Model Rules of Professional Conduct* identify five distinct roles that lawyers perform: advising, mediating, evaluating for the benefit of third parties, negotiating, and advocating. (See Appendix E.) Frequently, people, including lawyers themselves, think of lawyers primarily in terms of advocacy. As this section indicates, lawyers perform a number of distinct roles. In addition to the roles articulated in the *Model Rules,* two other important roles are those of agent and fiduciary.

The Lawyer as Advisor

At a very basic level lawyers give advice to clients. When a client asks, "Should I sell my business?" the lawyer may answer "No." This response should be more than a casual opinion. It should reflect the lawyer's experience and familiarity with the law, necessary research, legal analysis, and unbiased opinion. Legal advice according to the *Model Rule* 2.1 (See Appendix E) may include social, moral, economic, and political, as well as legal considerations.

Lawyers give advice all the time in virtually every client consultation. Some attorneys serve exclusively as advisors to their clients. Why is a lawyer's advice so valuable? In part, it incorporates legal considerations into the problem-solving process and few problems do not have some legal ramifications. Also, a lawyer's advice incorporates legal analysis that tends to focus on critical issues and viable solutions. Significantly, lawyers who do not practice law often continue in the role of advisor.

Another aspect of the role of advisor is counseling. The term "Attorney and Counselor at Law" denotes the fact that lawyers are counselors. Looking at the finer shades of meaning, the word advisor suggests directive communication from advisor to advisee, while counselor implies an interactive counseling process. Although the terms are often used interchangeably, the counseling process may be said to incorporate advising with active listening and fact gathering. Counseling also may refer to a licensed profession that deals with individuals who have psychological problems. Some lawyers may be licensed professional counselors and engage in therapeutic efforts to help their clients. Most, however, do not view themselves as trained psychologists by virtue of going to law school.

The Lawyer as Mediator

The concept of mediation is that the lawyer is counsel to the situation. In other words, he represents the interests of all the parties, but does not serve as advocate for any party. For example, two companies considering a merger may retain an independent mediator rather than separate advocates. As the demand for nonjudicial dispute resolution grows, the need for lawyers to serve as mediators also increases. Arbitration is a form of mediation in which the parties agree in advance to settle a dispute through an independent arbitrator whose role is somewhere between that of a mediator and a judge. Many labor–management disputes are settled through arbitration, but the process has been utilized in many other fields as well.

The Lawyer as Evaluator

Lawyers are often asked to evaluate a client's financial status, legal claim, or other matter for the benefit of a third party. Some examples of this role include certifying title of real property for a prospective buyer, issuing an opinion letter on a point of law to support a client's position in dealings with others, certifying a client's business position for Securities and Exchange Commission filings, and preparing federal or state income tax returns. In such situations, the lawyer not only has a duty to her client, but also to those for whom the evaluation is prepared.

The Lawyer as Negotiator

Because lawyers represent clients whose interests differ from those of others, negotiation is an important function in all forms of law practice. Lawyers are trained to argue, persuade, and communicate positions on behalf of their clients. Many legal disputes can be settled short of trial through effective negotiation. Often the parties have no intention of going to court, as, for instance, in salary negotiations between an athlete and a professional sports team. One way to think of negotiation is that it is like a pickup game of basketball where the players call their own fouls, compared to a trial where there is a referee. Negotiation requires strong interpersonal skills, an ability to compromise at the right time, a talent for quick response to changing situations and basic bargaining savvy.

The Lawyer as Advocate

When most people think of lawyers, they conjure up the image of an advocate. An advocate is someone who is trained to represent another before a tribunal. A tribunal may be a trial or appellate court, an administrative agency, a legislative body, or some other authority. A lawyer might represent an individual, a corporation, or the state. In every situation, however, the lawyer's job is to argue the client's position and to persuade the tribunal of the correctness of that position. In Anglo-American law, the roots of the modern trial lawyer grew out of the need for Anglo-Saxon peasants to be heard in the French-speaking

Norman courts. In other cultures the same idea emerged, that anyone facing a tribunal would be better served by hiring someone trained in persuasion and the rules of the court than by representing himself.

The Lawyer as Agent

One central element of the lawyer-client relationship is agency. An agent is one who is empowered to act on behalf of another. This power, or authority, is granted to the agent by the person who wants something done, the principal. In a lawyer-client relationship the client is the principal and the lawyer is the agent. When authority is properly granted to an agent by a principal, the principal will be bound by the agent's actions. For instance, if a client authorizes her lawyer to settle her civil dispute for any amount up to $50,000, the lawyer may settle the case for $45,000, but not $55,000. In numerous situations involving both negotiation and advocacy, this agency relationship is important because the lawyer acts independently from the client's direct control. Since the lawyer must utilize independent professional judgment, the client inevitably hands over authority to the lawyer. In this sense, the relationship is one of trust.

The Lawyer as Fiduciary

A special form of agency is the fiduciary. A fiduciary is someone who occupies a special position of trust with respect to the affairs of another. Fiduciary relationships may be found when a lawyer acts as a trustee, guardian, executor, or other position of special responsibility for a client's affairs. The client frequently has a diminished capacity to protect his own interests and must rely on the fiduciary to protect them. A fiduciary is held to an even higher standard of care than ordinary reasonableness in carrying out this role. Additionally, whenever lawyers hold clients' money or property their responsibility is a fiduciary one (*Model Rule* 1.15, See Appendix E).

WHAT LAWYERS DO

This section identifies a number of types of practice that describe the way in which lawyers work. In England, the bar is divided between barristers (litigators) and solicitors (office practitioners). America never adopted such a bifurcation. Over the years, however, the legal profession in this country has developed several distinct forms of practice (all of which might be pursued under the roof of a single office). Readers will note the parallels between the roles discussed above and these practice types.

Transactional Practice

A transactional practice is basically a non-litigation office practice. The best way to conceptualize this kind of practice is that it is one in which a client brings a specific transaction to handle: a will, a real estate closing, an incorporation, an adoption. In a transactional practice there is often no adversary in the sense that there would be in a lawsuit, although almost any transaction has the potential to end up in litigation. A simple probate may end up in court because the heirs challenge the will or disagree with its interpretation. A contract may produce litigation when it is breached by one of the parties. The transaction, however, is the original event handled by the lawyer.

Although some transactions may be incredibly complicated (e.g., making a movie), normally there is a beginning and an end to the case. The lawyer may be required to produce certain documents (or a single document), to file particular papers, to conduct specified research and render advice, or to counsel a client on the resolution of a problem. Mediation, evaluation, and negotiation can all be utilized in a transactional practice. Lawyers who engage in transactional practice often do not litigate cases, and vice versa, although many general practitioners do both.

Representative Practice

In a representative practice, a lawyer performs legal work for a particular client on an ongoing basis. Although the nature of the work may involve transactions or litigation, the key here is the continuing nature of the representation. Typically, a lawyer on retainer (an advance payment to secure the lawyer's services) makes herself available to the client for advice. The client may turn to the lawyer regularly or intermittently, but the lawyer will be prevented from representing others whose interests are adverse to those of the client.

Even in the absence of a formal retainer, some relationships may be so well established that a continuing representation exists. Another situation involving this kind of relationship may arise when a client buys 100 percent of a lawyer's or a firm's time. Thus, in-house counsel for corporations and government lawyers whose roles are primarily advisory may be viewed as representatives. The same may be said about sports or theatrical agents. Representative lawyers frequently engage in lobbying before legislative bodies, appear before administrative agencies, and make public comment on behalf of their clients. Representative lawyers often conduct negotiations or other work as agents for their clients. Increasingly, lawyers who work regularly for corporations and other clients are charged with the job of managing outside litigation counsel on behalf of the client. The in-house lawyer may not be a trial lawyer personally, but will retain, coordinate the activities, and review bills of lawyers who are. Although representative lawyers are not as visible as others, many times their efforts are overlooked by those unaware of the importance of such behind the scenes work.

Litigation

Litigation or trial practice is a broad category of practice that cuts across a wide range of legal work. In theory, almost any dispute or representation could go to court. Litigation is really a forum for dispute resolution in cases where no other approach has proved successful. Litigation is expensive, stressful, and time-consuming for lawyers and clients alike. The results are anything but certain; if they were, the case probably would have settled.

Litigation is normally divided along criminal-civil lines. Criminal litigation involves prosecution by the state for violation of the law (See Chapter 9). Civil litigation, on the other hand, includes all litigation that is not criminal. It is a much larger field, and much more difficult to encapsulate. The various chapters of Part II will address litigation within the context of various substantive areas.

There are basically three phases of litigation: pretrial, trial, and appellate. A lawyer may engage in all three, handling a case from beginning to end, or may specialize in a particular facet of the litigation process.

Pretrial litigation begins when a client first makes the decision to pursue a judicial remedy to a problem. At this stage the lawyer may advise the client on the desirability of pursuing a lawsuit, investigate the facts, research the legal precedents, prepare and file papers, and conduct discovery. Discovery is the pretrial process that allows opposing parties access to information about the other's case prior to trial. Discovery may involve depositions of key witnesses, interrogatories (i.e., questions) of the opposing party, or making available documents for inspection. Detailed rules govern the discovery process and the court may be involved in a series of pretrial motions and hearings. In addition to allowing each side to prepare its case, the pretrial process is designed to encourage settlement of conflicting claims.

Trial litigation is an art form of unique proportions. The image of the trial lawyer is most often that of a flamboyant, aggressive orator. In practice the key to successful trial work is more often careful preparation and organization than pure argumentation. The more famous trial lawyers such as Melvin Belli, Clarence Darrow, Racehorse Haynes, and Johnnie Cochran have a certain flair, but many other excellent trial lawyers quietly and skillfully win their cases on a regular basis.

A trial is like an extemporaneous play where the actors all have parts but the script is not written in advance. The outcome, too, is not decided until the final page. Essentially, each side is given a chance to present its case, challenge the case for the other side, and argue for a particular result. Whether the case is decided by judge or jury there is a special excitement in a trial. Some cases, particularly in the criminal area, generate a tremendous amount of public attention. In order to experience this drama firsthand, anyone thinking about attending law school should visit a trial personally.

Appellate litigation is a much more academic activity. After the trial court's decision, relying on the record of the trial below, the appealing party frames legal issues it believes were incorrectly decided. Both sides have an opportunity to present briefs and oral arguments, after which the appellate court makes a decision. Usually the court will affirm the lower court or reverse and remand for further consideration consistent with the appellate court's decision. Often, this means a new trial.

Planning/ Preventive Law

Another type of practice involves planning. By anticipating future legal problems it may be possible to avoid them or mitigate them. Since most people only visit a lawyer when disaster strikes (e.g., Uncle Harry dies without a will), preventive law has not attained the acceptance that perhaps it should. The concept of preventive medical care is widely accepted, but the idea has been slower to catch on in the legal sphere, especially among the working classes. Some of the areas of law where preventive practice is utilized are: estate planning, tax planning, business planning, and legislative planning. In these areas, lawyers may work with clients to identify particular objectives or to avoid certain difficulties, and then structure the client's legal affairs in such a way as to attain the client's goals.

Education

One of the least recognized types of legal work is education. The most obvious example would be a law school teacher, followed by a lawyer teaching at some other level of school or college. In fact, a substantial number of lawyers are employed in the educational field. But many practicing lawyers engage in teaching through client seminars, newsletters, public speaking engagements, and educating clients how to utilize self-help remedies to legal problems. Traditionally, lawyers' ethical obligations have included a duty to assist lay people to recognize their legal problems (See Appendix E, *ABA Model Code of Professional Responsibility,* EC 2–1). Thus, while teaching lay people about the law may be a type of practice for some, it is an avocation for many others.

Adjudication   A percentage of lawyers will become judges and participate in the litigation process as overseers and decision makers. Judges perform a central
role in the legal system, and the position has always carried with it a
special status of honor and respect. Although most judges do not reach
the bench until later in their legal careers, it may be useful to the prelaw
student to consider judicial work as a type of practice just like the others covered in this section.

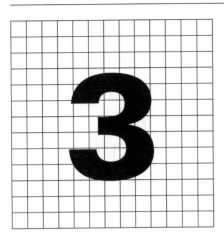

THE DELIVERY OF LEGAL SERVICES

The term *delivery of legal services* refers to the mechanisms by which legal services are provided to clients. In a broader sense, however, the issue encompasses all the different types of organizations in which lawyers work. This chapter explores many of these organizations. Because lawyers are employed in almost every imaginable environment, it would not be possible to describe them all. For instance, there is no chapter on lawyers who work as major league baseball managers, but at least one American lawyer, Tony LaRussa, has had that job. The categories listed here are those in which an identifiable number of lawyers work and provide law-related services.

PRIVATE PRACTICE

The largest single category of employment for lawyers is in the area of private practice. The term private practice refers to lawyers who provide legal services to clients for fees. In a free market economy lawyers sell their services to consumers of legal services. Rather than selling all their time to one employer, private practitioners make themselves available to a variety of different clients. Thus, private practitioners are entrepreneurs who must bring in more income in fees than the expenses of operating their offices. A law firm that does not make a profit will not remain in business long. Many lawyers have difficulty accepting the notion that law is a business, although it does not necessarily follow that law cannot be both a business and a profession. In fact, sometimes the demands of professionalism limit what lawyers can do as businesspeople. For instance, lawyers are prohibited from charging any fee that is not reasonable; otherwise they

CHART 2

Markets for Legal Services

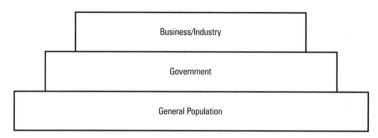

could charge any fee that the market would bear. These constraints help to define the legal services business as a profession within American society.

The *American Bar Foundation Lawyers Statistical Report* indicates that approximately 60 percent of all lawyers engage in private practice. This percentage has dropped steadily since World War II as more and more lawyers have joined organizations such as corporations and government agencies. A slightly higher percentage of recent graduates go to work in private practice after graduation. The National Association for Law Placement (NALP) Employment Report and Salary Survey has shown that over the past few years a consistent 65 percent of law school graduates go into private practice. An additional 12 percent serve as judicial clerks and a high percentage of those eventually enter private practice. This suggests that over the years there is some attrition from the ranks of law firms and individual practitioners. Indeed, many young lawyers find that they do not really enjoy practicing law. Other lawyers are hired by clients of the law firms where they work. Still others choose to enter public sector employment for some period of time. The idea that there is a revolving door in and out of private practice is anecdotally if not statistically verifiable.

The most high profile group of lawyers includes those who practice in large firms. The task of defining what is a large firm is made more difficult because firms are growing larger all the time. As recently as 1973, there were no more than 10 law firms in the U.S. with more than 100 lawyers. In 1991 there were over 250, and at least 3 with more than 1,000. This amazing growth has given rise to the term *megafirm.* Megafirms are highly institutionalized organizations that have frequently delegated many of the management responsibilities to nonlawyer professionals, leaving the lawyers to practice law. These firms operate out of several different offices in different cities, and offer a wide range of services to primarily large corporate clients.

Significantly, however, although the Bureau of Labor Statistics reports that Americans spend over 70 billion dollars annually for legal services, no single law firm accounts for more than 1 percent of that amount. This contrasts sharply with the experience of many other business and service industries including accounting where a handful of firms control 10 percent of the business or more. On the other hand, lawyers in the 100 largest firms account for only 5 percent of the lawyer population, but bring in 20 percent of the fees. Large firms tend to have the highest salaries for recent law school graduates, and for this reason competition for positions is intense. The demands on lawyers who work in large firms are heavy and the attrition great. For some Wall Street law firms in New York fewer than 1 lawyer out of 10 hired will eventually become a partner in the firm. Sometimes branch offices offer an interesting alternative for graduates who can be a part of the larger organization while working in an office that has the atmosphere of a smaller law firm.

Between the ranks of the very large firms and very small firms lies a group that defies definition. It includes the not-quite-megafirms in major cities—firms that for one reason or another have decided not to grow as large as their competitors or to branch out into other cities. It includes law firms that are the largest firms in many smaller cities—firms that represent a microcosm of the megafirms. These firms may be as small as 15 to 25 lawyers or as large as 50 to 100 lawyers. The limits of the category depend upon the size of the legal market in the city where they are located.

One thing is clear: somewhere between 10 and 25 lawyers, law firms begin to departmentalize. They subdivide along practice area lines. This shift transforms individual law practices into a group practice. Large law firms are in business to service the legal needs of large organizations. Not surprisingly, practice areas such as plaintiff personal injury, where most of the work involves one-to-one lawyer–client relationships, have never evolved into large organizations.

Medium-sized firms may be pubescent large firms; even the largest firms started out small at one time. They may be stable practices that have found a niche and do not want to grow. Or they may be the remnants of other law firms that have split up in the past. This segment of the market, while not highly visible, is a volatile one with changes occurring all the time.

Law firms are constantly undergoing change, as small firms grow into medium-sized and large firms, and large firms fragment or break up into numerous small firms. Lawyers themselves are likely to work in several different law firms over the course of their careers, and even a lawyer who stays in one place is likely to experience a series of metamorphoses over the years in the structure of his or her firm.

Many people would be surprised to learn that the largest part of the private practice field is comprised of small firms. Out of 40,000 law firms in the United States, only 2,000 have more than 10 lawyers. Despite all that has been written about larger law firms, the legal professional here remains one of very small practices. Statistics confirm this fact, indicating that nearly 20 percent of those entering private practice join very small firms. In addition, over time, many of those who begin their careers in larger firms will eventually choose the more intimate relationships afforded by smaller organizations as a place to pursue their livelihood.

Small law firms are less likely to depend upon large institutional clients for their business. They rely instead on "whoever walks through the door." Many of these firms are general practices in the sense that they service the legal needs of the local community. An increasing number of smaller firms, however, are becoming highly, if not exclusively, specialized. In terms of career opportunities, the chances are one out of three that students entering law school today will work for a law firm of fewer than 10 lawyers during their careers.

The last group of private practitioners are appropriately called *solos*. These lawyers practice alone with the exception of legal staff. Some solo practitioners may employ 10 or more support personnel who have not gone to law school, including paralegals, secretaries, investigators, and others. If the office is well organized, such an arrangement can be highly profitable. On the other hand, solo practitioners have the lowest per capita income of any group of attorneys.

Individuals may become solo practitioners for a number of reasons. They may enjoy the freedom of an entrepreneurial operation where they call all the shots. They may not want to be hassled or answer to other partners. They may not want to supervise or train associates. They may live in communities where there are simply not enough lawyers to form law firms. Surveys show that a high percentage of solo practitioners have been involved in a law firm at some point in their careers. Although they may eschew formal organizations, many solo practitioners utilize informal referral networks with other lawyers and, increasingly, participate in office-sharing arrangements in order to reduce overhead costs. Some commentators have suggested that the solo practitioner is a dying breed, since the percentage of solos has dwindled over the years: less than 40 percent of all lawyers practice alone and fewer than 5 percent of law school graduates elect to "hang out a shingle." At the same time, the actual number of lawyers who practice alone has in fact increased over the years.

CORPORATIONS

Corporation lawyers engage in a wide variety of activities from strictly legal work to exclusively nonlegal work and everything in between. The corporate lawyer, unlike the private practitioner, does not sell her services on the open market, but sells all her time to a single employer. In that sense, the corporate lawyer has only one client, the corporation. This relationship places unique ethical obligations upon a lawyer.

The largest number of corporation lawyers work as in-house counsel. Note the use of the term "corporation lawyers," in contrast to "corporate lawyers" who practice corporate law and may work either in a corporation or in private practice (See Chapter 7). In-house counsel are lawyers who practice law inside a corporation, typically in a corporate law department. One way to think of corporate law departments is that they are "kept" law firms. Like private law firms, law departments can range in size from one or two attorneys to several hundred. The role of the law department in the corporation also varies considerably, from providing advice to top management, to handling legislative work, to managing outside counsel, to providing full service in-house legal support. The use of in-house counsel grew dramatically through the 1980s, but corporate downsizing and restructuring has stifled the growth of law departments in the 1990s.

One common attribute of corporate law departments of all sizes is that they represent a cost rather than a profit center within the corporation. Since legal services represent a cost of doing business, a corporation must compare the cost of paying for legal services in-house to the cost of buying them from outside law firms. Most observers agree that general corporate legal services cost less in-house, although some specialized services requiring technical expertise may cost more. Whether a corporation uses outside or inside legal counsel may hinge on the amount of a particular kind of legal work that a corporation requires. Note that ethical rules prevent lawyers who work for corporations from offering services to clients of the corporation; the lawyers must advise the corporation alone.

The organizational structure of a corporate law department tends to be more hierarchical than that of a law firm. Usually, one general counsel, several associate general counsel, and layers of assistant general counsel work in a law department. Corporate salaries compare favorably with those in private practice. Although starting salaries for recent graduates may not be as high as for the largest law firms, they tend to be at or above the median for all law school graduates (approximately $40,000). Salaries for the general counsel and other high-ranking lawyers may be commensurate with salaries for the highest level executives in the corporation, and in many cases stock options and profit sharing can make such positions very attractive. There are, however, relatively few positions at the very top and the ceiling for corporate salaries is certainly less than it is in private practice.

Corporations, by virtue of their size, usually offer better benefits than law firms. This should not be surprising because the largest law firms are really very small business organizations. To the extent that benefits are related to the number of employees, corporations offer a flexibility that many law firms do not.

A second group of corporation lawyers include those who may be referred to as in-house lawyers. These individuals are not in a department because they are often the only lawyer in the company. They provide legal advice to management and frequently perform other managerial or administrative responsibilities. The companies that hire such lawyers are frequently very small, and the salary and the benefits are appropriately less. The advantage of such a position is that an individual may have an opportunity to grow with the company and eventually sit at the top of a large corporate law department.

A third group of lawyers who work for corporations do not practice law at all. These lawyers have gone completely to the management side of the business. They may be entrepreneurial individuals who have started the business alone or with others. They may have shifted from a law department into an executive role. They may simply have had an interest in business, and use law as a tool in their work.

GOVERNMENT

A third major employment category for lawyers is in government service. The *Lawyers Statistical Report* indicates that over 10 percent of all lawyers practice for some level of government. The *NALP Employment Survey* says that 10 percent of recent law school graduates accept government jobs. It is clear, however, that these are not always the same 10 percent, because of a phenomenon known as the "revolving door." The idea of the revolving door is that government and private practice lawyers go back and forth between the two types of employment for different periods during their careers. The lure of public service draws many individuals to the legal profession in the first place, and government service is a primary outlet for such public spiritedness.

In many instances government service also provides a greater degree of security and better working hours than private practice. On the other hand, the financial rewards of private practice exceed the opportunities in the government. For instance, a recent law school graduate can start working for the federal government at between $31,000 and $33,000. State and local government positions frequently pay less than federal ones. Top federal salaries, excluding high ranking political appointments, top out at close to $100,000. Such positions are also heavily weighted towards administration. In fact, as one moves up the government career ladder, it is reasonable to expect an increasingly large administrative component in the job. Those lawyers who enjoy practicing law more than managing people may want to shift to private practice rather than assume such management responsibilities.

Government practice frequently gives lawyers two important assets: expertise in a particular field of law and contacts that may be parlayed into clients in private practice. Ethical constraints may prevent the former government lawyer from representing individuals over whose matters that lawyer had responsibility in the government, but a lawyer's firm may be able to represent the client if the lawyer is effectively "screened" from contact with the clients.

The federal government is the largest subgroup of government service. Although federal government positions tend to be concentrated in Washington, D.C., government attorneys may work in regional offices throughout the country. The United States Justice Department may be the largest law firm in the world. It has one client—the United States—and although the department is divided into a number of divisions, most of the work involves litigation at some level. The Internal Revenue Service also employs a large number of attorneys, and special training in tax or accounting is a virtual prerequisite. A third major employer is the Treasury Department. In addition to lawyers with financial backgrounds, the Treasury Department includes the Federal Bureau of Investigation. Other departments with large legal staff include the State Department, Interior Department, Energy Department, Health and Human Services Department, and the Education Department.

In addition to the agencies just mentioned, attached to every United States District Court is a branch office of the United States Attorney. The U.S. Attorneys represent the prosecutorial arm of the federal government. In contrast, the Justice Department defends the United States when it is sued.

The military services also employ large numbers of attorneys, primarily in the Judge Advocate General's Corp. JAG officers are usually recruited directly from law school, although some officers may be sent to law school in return for a commitment to return to JAG corp service. JAG officers serve on military installations throughout the world, representing service men and women in cases from courts-martial to disputes involving civilian matters. Besides these military positions, the armed services employ a large number of civilian attorneys in areas such as procuring government contracts.

State governments have a variety of departments, many of which parallel offices in the federal government. Each state has an attorney general's office, tax division, education division, and other components analogous to federal agencies. The issues faced by state government lawyers may be more localized than at the federal level. There are also extensive opportunities for lawyers in positions that may not be restricted to lawyers, but for which lawyers are uniquely qualified, including administrative positions, hearings officers, and research analysis.

In the judicial branch, lawyers serve as judges, law clerks, and judicial administrators. Although most judges have been experienced and respected practitioners, some surprisingly young lawyers secure judicial appointments in a variety of lower level courts.

The institution of law clerking provides a postgraduate opportunity for new lawyers to learn the judicial system by working for a judge, conducting research and other forms of assistance. These positions provide young lawyers with an excellent credential along with a unique experience, and 12 percent of all graduates clerk for one to two years before moving on to other career opportunities. A smaller number of lawyers remain in the judicial system, not as judges but as professional managers.

A third level of government employment is in local agencies. All local political subdivisions at one time or another require legal representation. For small towns or counties, this work may be only part time; in larger entities, representation is handled by one or more full-time attorneys. In larger cities and counties, this office functions much like an in-house legal department in a corporation. The Office of the Corporation Counsel of the City of New York employs several hundred attorneys. Commonly, municipal lawyers are bifurcated along the same lines as the U.S. Justice Department and U.S. attorneys. That is, separate offices defend and represent the city or county in civil matters, and prosecute violations of the law in state or local courts. In addition to the positions enumerated above, there exist legal positions with many local boards and authorities.

A final category could best be described as quasi-governmental work. This includes hybrid agencies that constitute joint ventures between the public and the private sector. Although this tradition goes back at least to the New Deal and agencies like the Tennessee Valley Authority, such ventures gained prominence in the 1980s following the success of the 1984 Los Angeles Olympics. Because of their unusual status, these agencies often employ lawyers.

A significant number of lawyers work in the legislative branch of government at all levels. Although these positions do not technically require licensure as a lawyer, they have always attracted public-service-oriented lawyers. Not surprisingly, many lawyers will run for public office at some time during their careers. Congress, many state legislatures, and local councils are heavily represented by the legal profession. This has been the case from the period of the American Revolution to the present day. These elected representatives often hire lawyers to serve in staff positions as administrative assistants, legislative assistants, campaign managers, and public relations officers. Because the work of these aides frequently involves drafting legislation, interpreting government regulations, and representing the interests of the legislator and his or her constituents, legal skills fit particularly well into this type of work. One common career pattern is for a law school graduate to work as a legislative aide, move into a position with a government agency, and eventually enter private practice. The bulk of these positions are found in Washington, D.C., and the state capitals, although they exist in many larger cities as well.

NOT FOR PROFITS

A wide variety of organizations whose agenda involves the attainment of specific political action, law reform, or public interest goals, rather than profit, exist in and around the formal government bureaucracy. In truth, every political persuasion can and does utilize not-for-profit interest groups to influence legislation, conduct research, and serve the needs of its constituents. It is not inaccurate to say that America has become a nation of interest groups, and not for profits have increased dramatically in prominence. Lawyers, as might be expected, can be found throughout the fabric of this emerging area. Nonprofits include private associations, research institutions, think tanks, lobbying organizations, professional associations, citizen watchdog groups, campaign and fund-raising committees, religious and benevolent organizations, and related activities.

One particularly important hybrid organization is the Legal Services Corporation. Created by an act of Congress, the LSC consolidated many locally and privately funded legal aid organizations in the 1970s. The corporation provides legal services to Americans who could not otherwise afford representation and continues to carry this role today despite severe budget cutbacks during the Reagan and Bush administrations.

EDUCATION

The United States has a dual educational system consisting of both publicly funded and private institutions. Rather than listing education under either government or not-for-profit sections, it makes more sense to include a separate category. Lawyers are employed in all levels of the educational process from primary to postgraduate education. Law school teachers, of course, make up a major segment of the educational population. Many lawyers, however, are employed as college professors, high school teachers, and some even as primary educators. Still others work in administrative positions for educational institutions of all types. A small but notable group serve as university or school district counsel. A growing field is continuing legal education where lawyers provide adult and postgraduate education for other lawyers and nonlawyers alike. Many lawyers who do not work full time in the educational field participate as speakers for continuing legal education programs and informational seminars.

GROUP AND PREPAID LEGAL SERVICES

Group and prepaid legal services are relatively new legal services delivery systems. Group legal services are often provided through some trade or professional association such as a union. Lawyers for group members may be independent private practitioners or retained by the group to provide member services as a benefit. They are similar in concept to the medical HMO. Prepaid legal services, on the other hand, more closely resemble medical insurance. Under a prepaid plan clients would be reimbursed for legal expenses up to policy limits for specific kinds of legal services. A subscriber normally selects counsel of his choice, although many plans refer specific attorneys to their subscribers. During the 1970s, group and prepaid legal services plans were heralded as the key to providing affordable legal services to the middle class. For reasons that are not altogether clear, such plans have not been widely adopted, and many average Americans remain unrepresented until they are forced by crisis to seek legal assistance.

ENTREPRENEURS

A final group of lawyers go into business on their own. These entrepreneurs frequently utilize their legal skills in countless ways in forming, managing, and marketing their business activities. In many cases, it may be said that the entrepreneur as a businessperson is represented by herself, the lawyer. It would be futile to try to catalog the vast number of business ventures that lawyers pursue. Real estate and commercial development are common. Financial joint ventures also frequently involve lawyers. An increasing number of legally trained persons work as consultants, some providing highly specialized support services to other lawyers. Frequently these lawyers combine law and some other discipline to carve a unique market niche for themselves. For law firms trying to provide quality services to their clients, it is often easier to purchase expertise on the open market than to develop it in-house.

Writers

One entrepreneurial activity that seems to attract a large number of lawyers is writing. Most people do not realize the number of legally trained individuals throughout history who have become famous journalists, novelists, poets, and playwrights. In modern times, news reporting has proven not to be a particularly fertile field for legally trained minds. In part that is because legal analysis is particularly tuned to an approach that cuts quickly to the heart of the matter, analyzes it, and predicts outcomes.

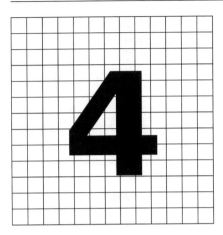

LAWYER DEMOGRAPHICS

Lawyers live everywhere. They work in cities, towns, and rural areas. By its nature legal work is concentrated in government and business centers. The following sections discuss the various settings where lawyers work.

POPULATION CENTERS

Approximately 88 percent of all lawyers practice in a major metropolitan area. This statistic reflects not only the broad twentieth century demographic trend of movement into the cities from rural areas, but also the reality that commerce generates legal business.

The largest legal markets are New York, Los Angeles, Washington, D.C., and Chicago. Washington, D.C., because of the many federal agencies in the city, can boast of the lowest ratio of population to attorneys of any city. New York has traditionally been the nation's legal hub, but California's growing economic clout and increasing population have propelled it into preeminence in the 1990s.

Other cities with significant lawyer populations include: Houston, Boston, Philadelphia, San Francisco, Atlanta, Denver, Dallas, and Miami. These cities for a variety of different reasons have established themselves as regional banking, industrial, governmental, transportation, or educational centers.

The remaining large metropolitan areas all have legal communities of substantial size by virtue of their population base. The cities of Detroit,

Cleveland, Minneapolis, St. Louis, Kansas City, Seattle, San Diego, Phoenix, San Antonio, New Orleans, Tampa, Baltimore, and Pittsburgh vary widely in geography, history, ethnic makeup, and economic base, but all represent an economic sphere of influence that extends far beyond the city limits.

In describing these legal communities by city, this book actually is referring to the metropolitan area. The concept of the SMSA (Standard Metropolitan Statistical Area) or CMSA (Consolidated Metropolitan Statistical Area—two or more SMSAs) provides a clearer picture of the scope of a legal community than just its center city(ies). Because many central cities have been engulfed by their suburbs, the population of the city does not reflect the true economic base of the SMSA. For example, Atlanta's population in 1988 was 420,220 while the Atlanta CMSA was 2,736,600. Houston's population of 1,698,020, on the other hand, dominates a CMSA of 3,247,000. Dallas-Ft. Worth CMSA is almost the same size as Houston's, but because there are two major cities in the CMSA, the city of Houston is much larger than either Dallas or Ft. Worth. Other bipolar CMSAs include: Minneapolis-St. Paul, Tampa-St. Petersburg-Clearwater, Kansas City, Missouri-Kansas, and San Francisco-Oakland-San Jose. An interesting demographic change on the East Coast involves the merging of Baltimore and Washington, D.C., into a single population center, popularly dubbed as Baltowash.

Many population centers have two or more commercial hubs. Even single city SMSAs like Atlanta, Houston, and Los Angeles have sprouted second downtowns in Midtown, the Galleria, and Century City respectively.

Most large cities—New York, Chicago, Los Angeles, and Philadelphia—include suburban cities that contain distinct legal communities. For example, Philadelphia is almost equidistant from Trenton, the capital of New Jersey, and Wilmington, Delaware, the "corporate capital of America."

Some other cities that have a very significant legal presence are either state capitals or the largest cities in their states: Austin, Albuquerque, Portland, Salt Lake City, Oklahoma City, Memphis, Indianapolis, Milwaukee, Columbus, Richmond, Birmingham, Hartford, Providence, Albany, and Sacramento. Like Washington, D.C., at a national level, state capitals attract a disproportionate number of lawyers, not only those who work for the state, but also those who represent clients engaged in lobbying and administrative (state) business. This is true even in smaller states.

A few cities that are neither the largest in their state nor state capitals have emerged as business-legal centers on their own: Buffalo, Jacksonville, Mobile, El Paso, Tulsa, Tucson, Nashville, Cincinnati, and Dayton. These cities may not challenge New York as the legal capital of the United States, but practice in such places represents a distinct alternative to the leading markets. These cities blend cultural opportunities and a high-level law practice with the lifestyle of a smaller city.

In most of the places described above, there are one or more major law firms with 50 or more lawyers, significant institutional clients, and/or government offices. It may be helpful to picture three separate legal markets: the general population, the government sector, and the business market (See Chart 2 in Chapter 3.). A city may have a greater or fewer number of lawyers depending on the mix of these three markets. The general population may require different numbers of lawyers depending on such factors as median age, per capita income, and specific legal needs. Government practice depends upon the size and number of government installations in a city. The business side is harder to correlate with the lawyer population. This is because the legal needs of business enterprises can vary widely by industry and events. The Exxon Valdez oil spill in Alaska, for instance, undoubtedly had an impact not only on the environment, but also on the legal needs of the Southern coast of Alaska as well. Some indicia of legal needs in the business community can be inferred from other statistics such as bank deposits, building permits, and retail sales.

The point of all this is that lawyers work wherever people live and work. And the more human activity there is, the more lawyers can be sustained. Lawyers may not always live where they work. Many lawyers who work in Washington, D.C., live in suburban Maryland or Virginia. For purposes of this discussion, such lawyers are Washington, D.C., lawyers, as opposed to Virginia or Maryland attorneys (who may live next door but also work in the suburbs).

Not surprisingly, the five most populous states have the five largest lawyer populations. These are California, New York, Texas, Florida, and Illinois. One out of ten Americans live in California, and almost one out of four live in one of these states. Figures for lawyers are similar, although California seems to have a disproportionate number of lawyers, perhaps due to the large number of law schools in the state.

The other geographic area that might be characterized as lawyer alley is the northeast corridor between Boston and Washington, D.C.—the most heavily industrialized part of the United States. Many demographers predict that eventually the entire corridor will be developed, and even now the gaps between the major cities are vanishing. Linked by highway, rail, and airplane service, the northeast corridor will continue to be home to large numbers of lawyers in the future.

SMALL CITIES AND TOWNS

Throughout the United States, there are countless smaller cities and towns, each with a unique legal community. These cities tend to serve as the economic hub of a smaller geographic area or even a county. These places might be home to a college (Athens, Georgia), an industry (Decatur, Illinois), or military installation (Bremerton, Washington). They may sit at some traditional crossroads (Natchez, Mississippi) or market (Lancaster, Pennsylvania). They may serve as home to a federal or state government complex (Dover, Delaware), or they may be a county seat. County seats tend to attract more lawyers than towns of similar size without the benefit of a courthouse.

These small towns and cities represent SMSAs of 50,000 to 250,000. In some cases, they may be considered a part of a larger CMSA. Yet these cities maintain their own identity and personality. The local bar is usually smaller numerically and per capita than in larger cities. The bar is also likely to be much more cohesive, because everyone knows everyone else. Deals are more likely to be done with a handshake. A large firm may have 10 or 15 lawyers. Lawyers may have to commute only 15 minutes to work and be able to see their families at night. Although the practice of law may not involve the same level of high stakes transactions or the same financial rewards, the tradeoff in terms of lifestyle is attractive to many. In today's world, there are few places that do not have relatively easy access to the fine arts, nightlife, restaurants, and other urban attractions. Residents of smaller towns, however, can go home and relax when they have had enough.

Some law graduates claim that it is difficult to find work or social acceptance in a small town if their parents and grandparents did not live there. While this may be partially true, newcomers may not bring with them the same historical baggage as longtime residents. For those willing to take the time to develop personal ties to an area, the opportunities are very real and the benefits notable. This life may not be for everyone, but for many lawyers, it is worth giving up the bright lights of the big city.

RURAL AREAS

Although the number of truly rural areas has dwindled over the past half century, rural life still exists throughout America. In the rural environment the principal industries—farming, ranching, logging, fishing—require space. The number of people per square mile is minimal and the towns are miles apart.

In rural areas the population of the county seat may be 10,000 or less, and the total population of the county less than 50,000 (and frequently smaller—the least populous county in the United States, Loving County, Texas, has fewer than 200 people). Small towns of several hundred to several thousand continue to serve as local markets and gathering places. Having been spared the major government and industrial complexes that have promoted the growth of their larger neighbors, these areas sometimes seem like lands that time forgot.

The bar in these small towns will be small and intimate with population-attorney ratios of 1,000:1 or greater. Bar associations of 10–20 attorneys are not uncommon, and some towns may not even have a single resident attorney. Still, the legal business gets done, some would say quicker and more efficiently than in the cities. Deals may be consummated over coffee at the local diner, and a lawyer's word is considered his bond. On the downside, lawyer income is likely to be less and legal work may be routine ("womb to tomb" as one small town lawyer quipped). Everyone knows everything about everyone else's business (and personal life). And the lack of access to cultural events may be oppressive to some.

If there is a segment of the population that remains under-lawyered, it is probably those who live in rural areas. Most law students come from urban centers and return to similar surroundings upon graduation. Even those who grew up in small towns frequently remain in larger cities after college and law school. This has resulted in a drain of talent, not just in law but in other professions as well, from rural areas. For those willing to make the commitment to this lifestyle, however, a satisfying future may lie in store.

LAW SCHOOLS

There are over 180 law schools in the United States approved by the American Bar Association, and several dozen more not approved by the ABA (See Appendix D). These schools produce over 40,000 graduates each year. Demographically, a significant portion of each school's graduates settle in the city where the law school is located. For those few schools that are not in any urban area, graduates often disperse to the closest local cities. The result of this trend is that cities with law schools usually have more lawyers than cities of comparable size without a law school.

Part Two
An Overview of
Major Practice Areas

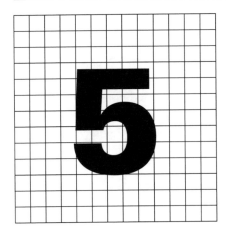

LEGAL SKILLS AND VALUES

What are the professional skills and values a lawyer needs to possess? Can they be learned or do they reflect innate abilities that are honed through education and experience? How does one acquire skills and values? Are there certain critical legal skills? Are some skills more relevant to success in practice than others? Do lawyers as a group share a set of basic values?

These are difficult questions and there are no easy answers. Certainly, many of the skills of lawyering are not the exclusive domain of lawyers (e.g., negotiating). And as this book has suggested, not all lawyers need to master the same set of skills. A number of basic skills contribute to success in many legal careers. These fundamental skills standing alone may not identify the attributes of every lawyer, but taken together they capture the essence of the successful lawyer in a variety of settings.

This chapter takes a look at skills from three different approaches. First, it covers skills in terms of a traditional career counseling model. Second, it addresses skills that contribute to professional success. Third, it considers skills in light of the findings of the ABA Task Force on Law Schools and the Profession: Narrowing the Gap. Finally, the chapter presents the related topic of shared professional values among lawyers. Together these materials define a composite picture of the skills and values that many lawyers need in order to perform their work competently. While no single list could comprehensively enumerate all the skills and values of lawyering, the reader may be able to discern enough common threads to be able to recognize and develop these attributes in his or her own career.

SKILLS

ABA Model Rule 1.1 says "A lawyer shall provide competent representation to a client. Competent representation requires the legal knowledge, skill, thoroughness, and preparation reasonably necessary for the representation." The term *skill* is the concept of professional competence, and is thus simultaneously linked to and distinguished from knowledge, thoroughness, and preparation. *Webster's New Twentieth Century Dictionary* (unabridged) defines "skill" as: "a great ability or proficiency, expertness."

One way to think of skills is that they represent *things that we do,* acts aimed at bringing about desired consequences. They are, in other words, action verbs; e.g., think, run, negotiate, argue. Skills may be simple (e.g., look), or complex, involving a set of numerous other skills (e.g., negotiate). They may be broad transferable skills (e.g., persuade) or career specific (e.g., litigate). They may represent innate abilities (e.g., analyze) or experience and/or education (e.g., study).

Career Skills

A number of career theorists from John Holland to Richard Bolles (author of the best-seller *What Color Is Your Parachute?*) hypothesize that all work requires the application of identifiable skills, and that different work requires different skills. Career theory also holds that people enjoy things they do well, and that they will do well in the future in activities utilizing the same skills they have employed successfully in the past. Conversely, when individuals lack the skills to succeed in an enterprise, they will not like the work. When such dissonance occurs, they will either change themselves (obtain the necessary skills), change the environment (revise the nature of the job), or leave the environment (find a new job).

Using this approach, an individual who can identify her own skills and the skills required in a particular career should be able to assess the likelihood of success in that field. In practice, most of us will like some aspects of our jobs but dislike others. Even people who hate their jobs usually enjoy some parts of their work. They usually have some, but not all, of the necessary skills. Sometimes people dislike their work although they are very skillful; these people often have work values inconsistent with those of their employers.

In one sense, only through experience, the application of skills in an actual work setting, can we know if we enjoy the work and if we are good at it. All planning, no matter how educated, is guesswork. We may be able to increase the probability of making sound career choices through good career planning, but we can never guarantee the outcomes.

Bolles identifies six major skill groups:

- Athletic
- Numerical
- Influencing
- Helping
- Creative
- Investigating

Different careers may require skills from each group differentially. For instance, lawyers more often use skills in the influencing group than in the athletic group. Obviously some lawyers will possess skills from groups less representative of lawyers as a whole. And some legal careers will tend to employ skills from different groups than others.

For someone contemplating a legal career, it may be important to decide whether his skill set corresponds to the general skill set of other lawyers. The process of analysis is beyond the scope of this book, but one can get help in this decision from a career counselor, a prelaw advisor, or some other mentor. Performance on the Law School Admission Test can be a useful indicator of legal aptitude. Work experience in a law firm or other legal employer may also prove useful. Other books by this author deal with aspects of the career choice process at different stages: *Barron's Guide to Law School* (the application process), *How to Succeed in Law School* (during law school), and *The Legal Career Guide: From Law Student to Lawyer* (the post–law school career search). Many psychometric profiles and other tests, such as the MBTI (Myers-Briggs Type Indicator) are utilized by both counselors and individuals considering law school. Although such instruments can help to clarify decision making, it is important to remember that they are tools and not necessarily predictors of success or happiness. For the present, this book focuses on making the decision to pursue a career in law generally, understanding that there are many different avenues for such a career to take.

Success Skills

In her 1978 book, *Skills for Success,* author Adele Scheele attempted to identify a set of skills that contributed to success among professionals. Her research, conducted on lawyers, suggested that a group of lawyers identified by their peers as "successful" possessed a number of important skills that helped them to be "in the right place at the right time." They didn't get more or better opportunities than others; they simply recognized and exploited them. These skills included self-awareness, networking, and positioning.

To the extent that one contemplating a career in law can begin even now to exercise Scheele's success skills in a meaningful way, it may be possible to maximize long-term career opportunities. Remember that there is not some great divide separating pre-legal from legal life, but rather there is a continuum of experience that flows uninterrupted through life.

Competence Skills

The skills that contribute to *legal competence* have been as hotly debated in the legal profession as has the term *competence* itself. Although a number of bar association committees and commissions have addressed the question of legal skills, The ABA Task Force on Law Schools and the Profession: Narrowing the Gap, has produced the most impressive and useful work. This task force, created by the ABA Section of Legal Education and Admissions to the Bar, and chaired by Robert MacCrate, of New York City, another former ABA President, was comprised of a blue ribbon panel of educators and practitioners. Among their objectives was the identification of the fundamental skills and values necessary for the practice of law. This information could be utilized in legal education and the profession to prepare lawyers better to serve their clients.

The Task Force Report contains the *Statement of Fundamental Lawyering Skills and Professional Values.* The insights are so incisive and its scope so broad that is offers an invaluable look at legal skills to those considering a career in law. The SSV, as it is called, breaks down legal skills into ten subdivisions (values are covered later in this chapter). These skill groups include problem solving, legal analysis and reasoning, legal research, factual investigation, communication, counseling, negotiation, litigation and alternative dispute resolution procedures, organization and management of legal work, and recognizing and resolving ethical dilemmas.

- *Problem solving* involves identifying and diagnosing problems, generating alternative solutions and strategies, developing a plan of action, and implementing the plan.

- *Legal analysis and reasoning* includes identifying and formulating legal issues, formulating relevant legal theories, elaborating legal theories, evaluating legal theories, and criticizing and synthesizing legal argumentation.

- *Legal research* incorporates knowing the nature of legal rules and institutions, knowing how to use fundamental tools of legal research, and understanding the process of devising and implementing a coherent and effective research design.

- *Factual investigation* requires determining the need for such investigation, planning an investigation, implementing an investigative strategy, memorializing and organizing information in accessible form, deciding when to conclude the process, and evaluating the information that has been gathered.

- *Communication* consists of effectively assessing the perspective of the recipient of communication and utilizing effective communication techniques.

- *Counseling* is the process of understanding the nature and bounds of the lawyer's role in the counseling relationship, gathering information relevant to the decision to be made, analyzing the decision, actually counseling the client, and understanding and implementing the client's decision.

- *Negotiation* incorporates preparing for the negotiation, conducting the negotiation, and counseling the client about the terms obtained from the other side.

- *Litigation and alternative dispute resolution procedures* both implicate problem-solving techniques requiring knowledge of the fundamentals of trial litigation, appellate litigation, advocacy in administrative and executive forums, and proceedings in other dispute resolution forums.

- *Organization and management* takes in formulating goals and principles for effective practice management, developing systems and procedures to ensure that time, effort, and resources are allocated efficiently, creating systems to ensure the timely completion of work, implementing systems for working with other people, and establishing procedures for efficiently administering the law office.

- The final category of skills addresses *ethical issues,* including familiarity with the nature and sources of ethical standards, understanding how ethical standards are enforced, and recognizing and resolving ethical dilemmas.

The SSV discusses all these skills in considerable detail, and offers suggestions for practitioners and educators. The document tends to provide a practice-oriented focus, and may not address some of the skills required in peripheral fields, or special skills necessary for specialized practice areas. As an overview of the general skills of lawyering, however, it is a useful device.

VALUES

Values deal more with what we believe than what we can do. Values include not only personal morals, but also attitudes toward work and relationships, and shared professional values. When it comes to work and personal values, lawyers represent a broad spectrum of attitudes. Research on work values suggests that there are identifiable profiles for *typical* lawyers and categories within the profession. Note the emphasis on *typical;* these studies are normative, and many successful lawyers do not fit the mold (e.g., for trial lawyers or patent lawyers). Shared values identified by the ABA Task Force were: providing competent representation; promoting justice, fairness, and morality; striving to improve the profession; and professional self-development. Although there may be other values than these that characterize lawyers generally, the SSV identifies a core group of lawyer values. In one sense the process of legal education inculcates these values, although in another sense many personal values are instilled long before law school.

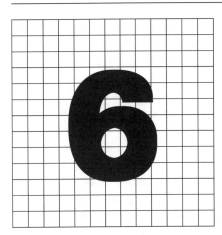

CAREER PATHS IN LAW

Much of this book deals with careers for lawyers. It should be apparent, however, that there are careers in law for persons who are not legally trained, and that there are opportunities outside of law for those who have gone to law school. These different types of positions can be referred to as *paths* because they represent a particular direction involving positions requiring similar qualifications. Although certain activities are limited to persons licensed to practice law, many law-related positions are open to both lawyers and nonlawyers.

In this chapter, the focus will be on different types of positions in law. The material is divided according to paths within the legal profession (for both lawyers and nonlawyers), paths in law-related enterprises (for either), and nonlegal positions for lawyers. This path approach may lead the reader to view the topic of legal careers somewhat differently.

PATHS WITHIN THE LEGAL PROFESSION

For Lawyers

Lawyers, as demonstrated already, practice in a variety of different settings. In all these settings, the work may be categorized as unsupervised, supervisory, and supervised. This characterization may be more meaningful than a simple partner–associate or owner–employee dichotomy. In the corporate, government, and other sectors, general counsels, managing attorneys, assistant general counsels, and staff attorneys replace partners and associates. Even in law firms, new categories of lawyers have been created to reflect the changing nature of the law firm pyramid: nonequity partners, permanent associates, and of counsel lawyers.

It may help to describe lawyers' work in three categories: unsupervised, supervisory, and supervised. It is possible for a single lawyer, at different times, to work under each of these circumstances. Unsupervised lawyers work independently for their clients. There is a direct attorney-client relationship. The lawyer's loyalty to the client, promise of confidence, and duty to act zealously flow directly from the relationship. The lawyer personally handles the client's work, offers advice, and represents the client's interests. These elements exist whether or not the lawyer works in a private firm, and whether or not the attorney is compensated.

Supervisory attorneys may maintain a direct relationship with the client, may handle parts of the work personally, and may be supervised by other attorneys. They may also delegate some or all of the clients' work to other attorneys. Supervisory attorneys are responsible for the quality of supervised work, the ethical behavior of the attorneys they supervise, and the timeliness of the legal product. In all but routine or simple legal work some supervision is required. Different skills are required in order to be a good supervisor as opposed to handling legal work with help. In addition to supervising other attorneys, the supervisory function also entails supervising the work of nonlegal support staff.

Supervised attorneys work under the direction of more senior lawyers. They may or may not have direct client contact but, in any event, their authority is derivative of the lawyer with whom the client relationship exists. This distinction is sometimes blurred where the law firm itself as an institution represents the clients. The distinction may also be difficult to make in large or complex cases where some lawyers are both supervisors and supervised. This arrangement is common in corporate law departments. Remember, however, that no matter how many lawyers are involved in the case, some lawyer at the top must be in charge of the representation and responsible directly to the client. The supervised attorney must complete the work according to the directions provided. The degree of independent work may vary widely from representation to representation. One significant aspect of the supervised attorney's work is the ethical obligation under the *Model Rules of Professional Conduct* (See Appendix E, Rule 5.2) to exercise independent judgment regarding ethical conduct. If the ethical question is one over which reasonable minds could differ, the supervised lawyer should follow the course recommended by the supervisor, but if the supervising attorney is clearly requesting the subordinate to carry out conduct that would be improper ethically, the subordinate must refuse to comply. In other words, the junior lawyer must disobey his boss if the boss asks him to do anything clearly unethical.

In general, supervisory and unsupervised work is handled by more experienced attorneys, while lawyers with less experience are supervised. Many new lawyers may be required to handle unsupervised work. Someone who hangs out a shingle after law school may not have the benefit of senior lawyers to oversee her work. One lawyer known by the author started work at a large urban district attorney's office after passing the bar. When he arrived for his first day on the job, he found a stack of files on his desk and learned that he would be in court at 10:00 that morning. Such a scenario is not uncommon. The question is properly raised whether these lawyers can competently handle unsupervised work at that point in their careers. Such a sink or swim approach, unfortunately, has permeated post-law school legal training. It is also not uncommon for very experienced lawyers to work in supervised situations, particularly in complex cases. In fact, a single lawyer may be involved as a subordinate, unsupervised, and supervisory lawyer in different cases at the same time.

The normal progression of work is to handle supervised work, move on to unsupervised work (because cases small enough for one lawyer to handle are inevitably simpler than multi-lawyer matters), and then to assume supervisory positions in bigger cases. Partners, associates, and other classes of lawyers may engage in any of these three tracks of work.

A small percentage of lawyers who work inside the formal legal profession do not practice law. These lawyers serve as administrators, teachers, judges, librarians, and technical advisors. They may or may not have moved from positions that involved delivering legal services to positions supporting the delivery of legal services. For example, the managing partner of a firm may not have time to practice law any more while the firm's librarian (also a lawyer) has never practiced law.

LAW-RELATED PATHS

There are many occupations that can be described as law-related because they involve working with the law or with lawyers. Jobs in these fields often can be filled by either lawyers or nonlawyers. The pros and cons of the relative merits of each are beyond the scope of this book. Each has advantages and disadvantages. Many activities can be characterized as practicing law when handled by a lawyer, but as something else when done by a nonlawyer (e.g., negotiating labor agreements). The list below is intended to be representative rather than inclusive.

Some law-related businesses are: accounting, sports and theatrical agency, title insurance, casualty claims adjustment, trust administration, stock brokerage, private investigation, economic and market research, petroleum land management, publishing (especially legal materials), teaching, and consulting. Fields such as mediation, arbitration, negotiation, and professional counseling also utilize both lawyers and nonlawyers. In recent years, a number of cottage industries have emerged to support the larger legal services industry: printing and copying services, temporary services, process servers, court reporters, heir location services, title searchers, surveyors, and many others.

The points are these: First, one can be involved in law without going to law school, or as a lawyer remain involved in the law without practicing. Secondly, for the entrepreneurial-minded individual, there are fascinating opportunities to identify a market niche in some law-related enterprise and pursue a career outside of traditional law practice.

NONLEGAL PATHS

Many lawyers never practice law; some never planned to, while others discovered during law school that law practice was not for them. Many practicing lawyers leave the practice of law; some find out that they do not enjoy practicing law while others are lured away by unique business opportunities and investments. A few lawyers straddle both the legal and nonlegal worlds. Author Scott Turow reportedly worked on his novels, *Presumed Innocent* and *The Burden of Proof,* riding a commuter train from the suburbs to his legal job in Chicago.

It would not be possible to catalog or classify all the different things lawyers do outside the law. Their activities are as varied as society itself. As a group, lawyers have disparate interests, at least in part because there is no single standardized path to law school. It is also the case that a legal education is an excellent preparation for much more than practicing law. Some law students feel obliged to practice law after attending law school. They should not; rather they should recognize the extensive opportunities that law school has created.

Nonlawyers

The roles for nonlawyers in organizations that provide legal services are extensive and growing. Before discussing specific nonlegal work in these organizations, it may be useful to look briefly at the changing nature of law practice in order to better understand this growing demand.

The practice of law is changing as discussed in Chapter 1. As lawyers form larger practice groups, whether law firms, law departments, or office sharing arrangements, they require larger support staffs. This is due in part to the greater complexity of the organization. It is also a product of economies of a scale that allows large organizations to have in-house services that must be purchased on the open market by smaller groups. For instance, a solo practitioner probably would not need a full-time law librarian, but a shared office suite of thirty attorneys might. Another reason for this development is the growing complexity of practice itself. Legal services can be delivered more efficiently by a team of professionals, paraprofessionals, and support staff than by a lawyer alone. Legal advice is often colored by economic, social, moral, and other issues that require nonlegal expertise.

Another important change in law practice is the willingness of lawyers to delegate management chores to nonlawyers, freeing the lawyers to practice law. Traditionally, even in the largest firms, practitioners held onto all decision-making authority. More and more lawyers are realizing that when they are running the law business they are not handling the law practice. The recognition that they can hire people who are not lawyers to manage the organization has led to greater opportunities in law practice for nonlawyers.

These paths may be categorized as professional, paraprofessional, and support staff. Although the dividing lines are often unclear, there is a general division between employees who are covered by the federal Fair Labor Standards Act and those who are exempt. Support staff such as secretaries, receptionists, file clerks, and other clerical workers are protected by the Act. The FLSA sets minimum wages and requires that employees who work over forty hours per week be given overtime pay. These provisions apply whether the firm calls employees' pay "salary" or "wages."

Professional employees are said to be exempt from the Act, and although these workers normally have more demanding, higher paying jobs, they are not afforded the same protection as clericals. Since very few law offices are unionized, office workers, particularly professionals, have few job guarantees. Paraprofessionals may or may not be exempt from the FLSA, depending on their job descriptions, qualifications, and pay structure. If the term paralegal is merely a different name for a secretary (or as one office manager said, "A paralegal is a secretary who can't type."), then legal assistants probably will be covered by the FLSA. If they have specialized responsibilities, independence in making decisions, and college level training or certification, they are more likely to be considered exempt. In terms of career opportunities for college graduates, exempt positions are more likely to be appealing than those covered by the Act.

Professional employees can include a number of top level managers: the law firm administrator or office manager, director of personnel, recruiting director, law librarian, MIS (management information systems) director, marketing director, salary and benefits administrator, educational director, and accountant. Some firms hire specialists to work directly with the legal services delivery team (as opposed to supporting it administratively), such as investigators, researchers, analysts, and even experts (e.g., a doctor or an engineer). Some firms create ancillary business ventures (e.g., consulting firms) to allow these professionals to operate independently while serving the firm's needs. Professional staff until recently could be found only in very large firms and departments, but the trend is for the practice to filter down to smaller and smaller organizations. There are growing opportunities for business, computer science, human resources, marketing, and accounting majors in law, as well as for librarians, economists, statisticians, and other specialists.

Paraprofessionals, or legal assistants, work directly with attorneys in delivering services to clients. They typically handle routine aspects of the practice such as basic document assembly, docket and calendar management, simple research, standardized interviews, and other specialized, regular tasks that the lawyer may delegate. Since the lawyer is ultimately responsible for the work product, the paralegal's work product is normally reviewed by the attorney, although the work itself may be performed independently. In addition to graduates of accredited paralegal schools, some firms draw their legal assistants from the ranks of college graduates in social sciences, English, and other liberal arts fields.

Support staff positions offer the least pay and status in the world of law practice, but remain as options for those interested in a career in law who do not have seven or eight years to go to law school or even four or five for business school. Additionally, support staff and paralegal positions have long been an excellent way to pay for law school while working during school in a law-related job.

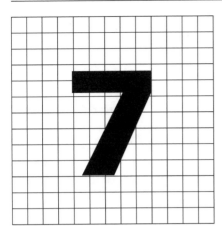

BUSINESS LAW

The broad heading of business law encompasses an unusual diversity of different but related types of practice. Since the industrial revolution, the size and complexity of the business world has continued to grow. Advances in communication and information technologies have accelerated the pace of change. In its simplest sense, business law seeks to establish workable, reliable rules for those who engage in commerce or business (those who buy or sell goods or services). Businesses to a greater extent than individuals rely upon legal services to attain their objectives, protect their interests, and vindicate their rights. As mentioned in Chapter 3, business law creates a demand for legal services far above individual demand for such services in the general population. Business law is concentrated in industrial and commercial centers, although it is present to some extent everywhere. This chapter only highlights the most important areas within the larger field.

CONTRACTS

General

Generally, contract law involves the formation and enforcement of agreements between parties. Basic principles of contract law take up a full course in the first year of law school and require coverage in many other law school classes. Most contract practice can be said to fall under three major groupings: contract formation, contract interpretation, and litigation for breach of contract. People make contracts because they think they are getting a good deal. They break contracts when the deal turns sour. There are all kinds of contracts, but several deserve special mention because they have created their own specialties within the law.

Insurance

The first of these is *insurance law*. Perhaps no other field has so dominated the business world; to paraphrase Shakespeare it stands astride the business world like a colossus. Insurance involves paying premiums to an insurer to protect against the occurrence of specified risks. Whether the risk is the premature death of a policyholder or the possibility of injury to a visitor on someone's property or the chance that a product may injure its ultimate user, insurance has proven to be an effective protection against catastrophic loss.

At the same time, insurance is at the root of much litigation today. Patients who sue their doctors for malpractice, for instance, are in most cases seeking recovery from the doctor's insurance carrier. For many injuries, the responsible individual or company lacks the assets to fully compensate the injured party, who then looks to the "deep pocket" of the insurance company. The insurance policy is a contract between the policy-holder and the insurance company whereby the insurer, in return for the payment of premiums, promises to pay a designated amount if the covered risk actually occurs. Although many lawyers work in-house for insurance companies, the largest segment of insurance practice involves litigation.

Lawyers may practice insurance defense (representing insurance companies) or represent plaintiffs (parties who claim that a policy-holder has harmed them). (See also Chapter 21.) Despite numerous exceptions, lawyers tend to remain on one side of the docket or the other. The high cost of insurance and the increase in litigation have produced periodic calls for reform in the way risks are protected and losses compensated. Although the present system will undoubtedly undergo reform, the insurance system is so firmly entrenched in society that it is unlikely to disappear in the near future.

Construction

A second area that has attained specialty status is *construction law*. This field of law governs the building industry, one of the largest in the United States. In addition to property owners and developers, construc-tion involves architects, general contractors, subcontractors, suppliers, and government agencies that issue necessary permits and certifica-tions. The construction project may be a part of a large commercial real estate deal. Or it may involve a simple structure for an individual property owner (See also Chapter 18). Wherever the building trades are involved, however, construction law is implicated in defining the rights and duties of all parties to the construction project. Since the building process requires special understanding, the creation of a specialty in construction law was a natural development. Although many lawyers will be involved in a construction project at some time or another in their careers, only those with special knowledge and skills can handle particularly difficult, complex, or high-cost projects.

Franchising

Since World War II one of the fastest growing areas of contract law has been *franchising*. Countless businesses involving extensive products and services have been franchised in this country and around the world. This idea is simple. If you have a good product, let's say a hamburger, you might build and operate new branches of your hamburger emporium. As an alternative, you could sell the right to replicate your hamburger business to an independent owner who could benefit from your good name, marketing, and experience in making good hamburgers. This franchisee would open a business with a proven formula of success for a minimum amount of development costs and a reduced risk of failure. A drive down any strip highway in America will provide visual confirmation of the viability of this concept. What most observers do not see when they view the golden arches is the *legal work* that makes franchising possible.

BANKING

Banking law involves the legal problems of financial institutions, including commercial banks, credit banks, savings and loan institutions, and mortgage banks. The banking system in the United States is held together by the Federal Reserve Bank which controls the supply of money. On one hand, banks are charged with holding and protecting their depositors' assets; on the other, they are profit-making businesses that lend money to qualified borrowers in order to earn money. Banking law involves all of the intricacies of borrowing and lending and regulations involving movement of money through the system. The experience of the Great Depression reminds us that the banking system is a fragile one that requires constant fine tuning. In the midst of all this banking activity are lawyers who represent the banks, borrowers, customers, and regulators. Since the 1930s, government involvement in the financial system has been prominent. In recent years, lenders and creditors have been required by law to provide greater information to borrowers and to guarantee certain basic rights regarding banking and loan transactions.

CORPORATE LAW

The term *corporate law* is frequently used to describe not only the law involving corporations, but also partnerships, limited liability companies, and unincorporated associations. Corporate law may be practiced either in-house or by outside counsel. Under the rubric of corporate law, lawyers perform a number of specific functions.

Incorporation

Probably the most basic transaction in the life of any corporation is the incorporation of the company. The process of incorporation includes the reserving of a name, drafting bylaws, electing officers and directors, securing capital, and registering the corporation in the state of incorporation. In the case of a partnership, the lawyer may be required to draft a partnership agreement.

Advising

Next, there is the work of providing legal advice to the corporation for ongoing business activities. The nature of the advice will depend upon the nature of the corporation's business. A complicating factor concerns the lawyer's duty of loyalty. As counsel to the organization, the lawyer represents the entity rather than individual managers, officers, or directors. This responsibility can be confusing since the organization is a legal fiction that can only speak or act through one of its authorized agents. When the agent's conduct deviates from the best interests of the corporation, the lawyer must remember that the client is the organization and not the person.

Securities

A third area of corporate law involves securities—stocks and bonds. Securities raise capital for the corporation in return for an equity position in the corporation. Stockholders are the ultimate owners of a publicly traded corporation, while bond holders are more like lenders who get a predetermined return on their investment. The value of stock fluctuates with the market. Since the stock market crash of 1929 stocks and bonds have been closely regulated by the Securities Exchange Commission of the federal government. Any publicly held corporation, one that sells equity on the open market through a stock exchange, must file detailed legal documents with the SEC prior to any stock offering. This highly technical work requires a high degree of legal expertise. Bond lawyers are even more highly specialized than general securities lawyers.

Mergers and Acquisitions

Some of the most high stakes, fast moving, and pressure-filled legal work involves *mergers and acquisitions.* During the 1980s, free market opportunism produced cataclysmic activity. Corporate raiders, identifying target corporations with undervalued stock, engaged in a technique called *leveraged buyout* (LBO). An acquiring corporation using short-term financing secured by its own assets would offer to purchase large blocks of stock in the target corporation at a premium price. If the acquirer could amass enough of the target company's stock, it could obtain control of the company. The takeover attempt frequently drove up the stock price and hence the value of the target company. In a successful corporate acquisition, the acquiring company could pay off its short-term debt through the increase in the value of the acquired stock. If this did not happen, the acquiror would be forced to sell off assets of its own or of the acquisition, or convert its short-term debt to long-term debt. Although many of the abuses of the 1980s have subsided today, corporate takeovers still occur, as weaker companies are consumed by stronger ones.

Although many takeovers are hostile, unwanted by the target, others are friendly. *Corporate mergers* represent a variation on this theme. In a merger, two companies consolidate operations into a single entity. Such legal work is incredibly complex, and only a handful of law firms can offer services in this area.

International Commercial

An emerging practice area for the 1990s is *international corporate and commercial law.* International business transactions involving multinational conglomerates, cartels, and government supported industries in a changing international political atmosphere produce unique business and legal challenges for lawyers who represent clients in this area. The increasing interdependency of economies and international money management practices means that more and more lawyers will be engaged in international practice in the future. In prior years, international business was a very rarefied activity and a small number of law firms handled the lion's share of the work. As new markets have opened up abroad, the increased need for legal services simply cannot be handled by the old international bar. Whereas much of the international practice was traditionally controlled from New York City, a host of new international gateways has emerged; Miami, San Antonio, Los Angeles, San Francisco, and Honolulu.

REGULATED INDUSTRIES

A number of industries do not operate in a totally free market. They are subject to government regulation to protect the public interest. Each of these industries supports a specialized practice area involving lawyers in both government and industry who represent both the regulators and the regulated. Although government regulation of industries has declined in recent years, the economy is far from deregulated.

The first of these industries is utilities—gas, water, electricity, nuclear power, and telephone. While these public utilities are profit-making businesses, and not government owned as in many countries, they must seek approval for their rate structures from a variety of federal, state, and local commissions.

Transportation is another regulated industry. Common carriers such as trucking, railroads, and airlines that operate in interstate commerce used to be totally regulated. For instance, the Federal Aviation Administration gave out route and landing rights, set fares, and governed many other aspects of air travel. Airline deregulation eliminated protected routes and controlled fares. Other aspects of the airline business remain under the watchful eye of the government. As with the utilities, transportation involves lawyers on both sides of the regulatory process.

A third regulated industry is communications—radio and television. In the case of the broadcast media, the problem is that there are a limited number of broadcast frequencies. The Federal Communications Commission under the Federal Communications Act has the power to grant broadcast licenses in the public interest. Licensees must have their licenses renewed periodically and may lose them if they fail to meet FCC standards. As expected, much of the licensing process involves lawyers. On the other hand, the Internet and the cable industry are not regulated nationally. Because of First Amendment considerations, nonbroadcast media such as newspapers and film are generally exempt from the kind of regulation broadcasters encounter.

A final regulated industry is the area of food and drugs. The Food and Drug Administration (FDA) strictly controls the marketing and distribution of prescription and over-the-counter medicine. Before a medicine can be sold, it must be tested for effectiveness and side effects. The representation of pharmaceutical companies and other manufacturers of drugs falls to a specialized bar capable of taking such products through the regulatory approval process. Among the issues relevant to food distribution are product contamination and packaging. In recent years the question of labeling has become increasingly important. Agricultural businesses large enough to place products into the stream of commerce must meet strict government specifications, and lawyers inevitably represent food distributors in this process. Although the food and drug industries may be described as regulated industries, producers and distributors must be cognizant of product liability law if a product injures an ultimate user. Another area where regulatory concerns arise with regard to food and drugs involves the Federal Trade Commission, which regulates false, deceptive, and misleading advertising.

BANKRUPTCY/REORGANIZATION

One consequence of a free market system is that a certain percentage of all businesses will fail in any given year. During recessionary periods the failure rate is substantially higher. The likelihood of business failure is highest for newly created businesses rather than existing ones. Bankruptcy law has evolved as a highly specialized branch of commercial law governed by the U.S. Bankruptcy Code. Generally, when an individual or business cannot meet its financial obligations, the Code can be used to protect debtors from their creditors while seeking to secure the ultimate payment of the debts. During the pendency of a bankruptcy action, many of the usual laws involving creditors' rights are suspended. The bankruptcy system is administered by special administrative courts and judges. Bankruptcies can range from individuals with no assets and an inability to pay off credit cards to multimillion-dollar business collapses such as Eastern Airlines.

Not all businesses with financial problems are forced into dissolution. Many, under Chapter 11 of the Bankruptcy Code, are allowed protection from creditors while they reorganize to operate more profitably and ultimately fulfill their financial obligations. The use of bankruptcy as a defensive legal tool has increased under the provisions of the liberal Bankruptcy Act. Many otherwise healthy businesses with a short-term cash flow problem and no plans to shut down avail themselves of the reorganization provisions of Chapter 11. This branch of bankruptcy law sometimes known as "workout" has grown dramatically, particularly as the stigma associated with filing bankruptcy has diminished. A larger number of companies are also candidates for workout help than in the past.

The branch of bankruptcy practice that involves business failure is tied closely to the business cycle, but unlike areas such as real estate that improve when times are good, bankruptcy practice increases when the economy falters. A large business failure can involve complicated and protracted proceedings. When a company closes its doors and stops paying its bills, *everyone* who is owed money, from the office supply company to the mortgage banker, will be represented by counsel, and file liens against the assets of the defunct organization. The court establishes priority of liens (i.e., who gets paid first) and the payoff rate (e.g., fifty-five cents on the dollar). In many cases, the court will appoint a special trustee to represent the interests of the bankrupt organization and to negotiate a settlement with its creditors. The trustee is inevitably a practicing bankruptcy attorney, although a different one from those attorneys representing parties in the litigation.

ANTITRUST

In 1890, Congress passed the Sherman Antitrust Act, prohibiting business combinations or monopolies that restrained trade. The Sherman Act was a response to nineteenth century business practices that concentrated business capital in the hands of a few "robber barons" in many industries, men whose actions drove competing organizations out of business. Over the years, antitrust policy has evolved to apply to any organization or group of organizations working in concert to dominate an industry, fix prices, or restrain the free flow of products and services. Antitrust cases can be very large and last for years. Companies charged with antitrust violations are frequently among the nation's largest, and these companies possess vast resources with which to defend themselves. One of the most famous antitrust cases resulted in the breakup of AT&T, illustrating not only the magnitude of such cases, but also the consequences that antitrust litigation can have. The breakup of AT&T did not occur overnight; it took years of litigation involving the government, smaller communications companies, and AT&T. More recently, Microsoft Corporation has had to face a variety of antitrust charges from the government and competitors.

Until the early 1980s the United States Justice Department Antitrust Division was the most important player on the antitrust field. Large companies were defended by a small number of very large firms that possessed the resources required by antitrust litigation. Smaller companies were represented by a plaintiffs' antitrust bar that was much less clearly defined. With the coming of the Reagan administration's laissez-faire economic policies, the Justice Department became much less aggressive in the area of antitrust enforcement. Leadership of many antitrust cases devolved to the plaintiffs' antitrust lawyers themselves.

Since antitrust cases usually involve a large number of small plaintiffs, all represented by different lawyers against either one or a small handful of companies represented by no more than a few law firms, it was necessary for plaintiffs to develop some form of cohesive strategy. The courts, in effect, created *ad hoc law firms,* firms established for one case. One lawyer was usually designated to lead this ad hoc firm and coordinate plaintiffs' actions.

Similar steps have been taken in other areas involving *complex litigation* such as mass disasters, product liability, and bankruptcy. Out of this arena has grown a new specialty involving the management of complex litigation. It is one thing to direct the activities of one hundred lawyers in the same law firm; it is quite another to try to coordinate one hundred lawyers from one hundred different firms. In an international environment of increased complexity and open markets, the future holds a high likelihood that such complex litigation, in the antitrust field and elsewhere, will proliferate. While politicians may continue to debate the merits of such policies, the involvement of lawyers in business and the attendant litigation is unlikely to subside for the foreseeable future.

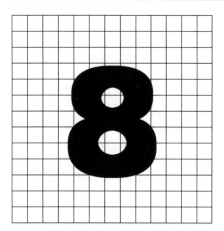

COMPUTER LAW

The technology revolution has ushered in a host of novel legal problems. The legal system is often ill equipped to cope with the many ramifications of technological change in society. Since much of the law and the legal system evolved during the Middle Ages, it should not be surprising that many traditional legal concepts do not translate easily into a post-industrial world.

This chapter will address various aspects of the law in a technologically-oriented society, legal issues that taken together have become identified as the field of computer law. Almost all lawyers have come face-to-face with the computer revolution in one way or another. Technological changes have totally restructured many aspects of the practice of law. Lawyers use computers for preparing documents, maintaining files, and developing cases for court. And technology appears increasingly as a factor in many legal cases.

What this means is that lawyers not only must understand the technology for themselves, but they must become involved periodically in technological issues on behalf of their clients. Thus, it may be said that every lawyer deals with computer law in some way at least periodically. Additionally, there exists a group of lawyers who practice computer law extensively or even exclusively. These lawyers often possess qualifications in other arenas such as information science, mathematics, engineering, or some other computer-related field, in addition to training in the law. Anyone contemplating a career in computer law should consider gaining educational credentials or practical experience in the computer industry to supplement a legal education.

Although the descriptions here are by no means exhaustive, they present an interesting overview of many of the problems that fit under the umbrella of computer law. Such classifications may seem somewhat arbitrary, but they provide a useful organization for the material in this chapter: computers in the courtroom, the computer industry, intellectual property, information resources, and criminal law. Criminal law and intellectual property law are covered in separate chapters in this book. Many aspects of law and the computer industry are business law problems with a technological twist and are addressed in the chapter on business law. There is also some crossover between other parts of computer law and traditional fields of legal practice. The differences are significant enough and the volume of work sufficient, however, to include the topic of computer law as a separate chapter.

COMPUTERS IN THE COURTROOM

The use of technology in a variety of ways by the judicial system has transformed not only the way courts do business, but also the way they address certain legal issues. The judge, for instance, may remain electronically connected to his law clerks and staff during trials, as a tool to manage the trial process more efficiently. Court reporters may now use voice recognition software and electronic data storage to improve the quality and reduce the costs of court transcripts.

Attorneys representing clients in court may use computers in trial preparation, including such tools as laptop computers on the table as they present their cases. Presentation software permits lawyers to develop charts, graphs, and other illustrations as demonstrative evidence. Some companies even specialize in creating computer animations, depictions of events in a case based upon factual evidence. The admissibility of such evidence, which can be very powerful in its effect on a jury, presents special legal problems for the court. Videotaped testimony of witnesses who for a variety of reasons cannot appear personally in court also raises admissibility issues in the law of evidence. Even the use of computers to analyze evidence, in such areas as statistical probabilities and DNA identification, could induce a level of sophistication and complexity to many trials that was unthinkable in former times.

Many courts now permit filing of papers and service of process to be done electronically. The inadvertent disclosure of privileged information caused by the misdirection of a fax or e-mail raises legal issues for the court as well. All these changes point to a judicial system in flux, one that is utilizing technology in a variety of ways and struggling to apply traditional rules of law in these new situations.

THE COMPUTER INDUSTRY

In some ways, the computer industry is like any other industry. Companies develop, produce, and market products for selected consumers. Successful companies are profitable and unsuccessful ones go belly-up. Yet the computer industry is special for a number of reasons. For one thing, many of the computer industry giants were started by youthful entrepreneurs with very little capital but a great idea and boundless energy.

The example of Microsoft Corporation is not atypical. Bill Gates and his high school friend, anticipating the computer revolution, dropped out of college in order to write operating instructions for the small personal computers that were just then beginning to appear in a market dominated by mainframes. They incorporated their business and aggressively courted hardware producers who needed operating systems to make their new personal computers marketable to the masses. Contracts were negotiated with IBM and Apple as well as other manufacturers to produce these systems, and the rest is history. Today, Microsoft is one of the most powerful companies in America, the largest producer of software in the world. In addition to engineers, programmers, researchers, and other workers, Microsoft also maintains an in-house legal department of over 100 lawyers and retains the services of a variety of outside law firms on a regular basis. These lawyers represent Microsoft on matters as wide-ranging as licensing of products, antitrust lawsuits by competitors, and labor relations problems within the company.

Although other computer companies are not as large as Microsoft, they have all relied extensively on legal services to grow from start-up businesses to industrial giants. It would have been very difficult for most of these businesses to achieve the success they have without the assistance of lawyers at every step. In turn, the lawyers who represent clients in the computer industry and who deal with issues of law and technology on a regular basis have become the core of the computer law field.

INTELLECTUAL PROPERTY

Intellectual property law generally consists of copyright, patents, and trademarks. Whenever one writes a book, invents a process or product, or develops a new process, that person often expects to see the fruits of her efforts in the form of a financial remuneration. People who write computer programs or devise other applications for technology expect to secure rights to their intellectual property. The problem with computers is that these rights, which were established for traditional written products and inventions, were often ill-suited for application in the computer industry because of the special nature of computer products. For example, the traditional protection for inventors, securing a patent, proved unwieldy in the computer area for many reasons. It took so long to secure a patent that in many cases the rapidly changing technology had become obsolete by the time the patent had been perfected. The topic of intellectual property rights in technological hardware and software is discussed more thoroughly in Chapter 15 on intellectual property law.

INFORMATION RESOURCES

As technology has advanced to allow for the storage and retrieval of vast amounts of information databases and global access to such information resources, the science of information management has become increasingly important. Professionals who are trained to manipulate and control this sea of information have particular value in society. Not only traditional librarians, but also a variety of system architects, consultants, and information specialists help people to locate and use the information they need. The legal profession is particularly information-based, and technology gives lawyers access to more information than ever before, but in order to use information, lawyers need to be able to find the information they need, and lawyers who specialize in information resources are becoming increasingly valuable to other legal practitioners.

Criminal Law

Computers and other forms of electronic technology have ushered in a host of new ways to commit old crimes such as fraud and some new ones such as theft of electronic information. Although criminal law is covered in Chapter 9, it is worth noting here that as long as there are people with criminal minds and those people have computers, there will be computer crimes, and there will also be lawyers who deal with the unique problems of technology and criminal law.

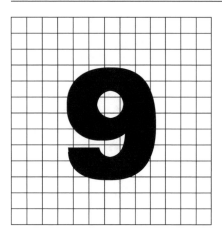

CRIMINAL LAW

Criminal law may be the most highly visible area of law practice. Americans have always had a fascination for high profile crimes. Even before the O.J. Simpson case, we were enthralled with the Lindbergh kidnapping and the Watergate Affair. Notorious criminals themselves such as Billy the Kid, Al Capone, John Gotti, and Jeffrey Dahmer are held by the public in macabre fascination. So, too, are the law enforcement officers like Wyatt Earp and Elliott Ness. And after the miscreants are brought to justice, the criminal trial can be just as intriguing. This drama has been played out in hundreds of books, movies, and television shows. One of the most notable was *Perry Mason,* the astute criminal lawyer who always managed to get his client off, while the hapless D.A., Hamilton Burger, could only shrug in frustration. The real life Perry Masons—Johnnie Cochran, Racehorse Haynes, Clarence Darrow, Percy Foreman, F. Lee Bailey, and others—may be as well known as some of their clients.

In reality, the criminal justice system does not usually proceed with such dramatic flair. Most cases are disposed of without a trial and those that go to trial result in a high percentage of convictions. This does not mean that some innocents do not go to jail; consider the true story depicted in the movie *The Thin Blue Line* where a black engineer was convicted of a murder he did not commit while the police held back exculpatory evidence. Or cases where the complaining witness years later recants the testimony that convicted the defendant. As we know, some culpable individuals are acquitted as well; the newspapers are full of stories about criminals who got off on a technicality. Despite its shortcomings, however, the criminal justice system works to punish antisocial behavior and to protect society from individuals who engage in such conduct. Criminal law practice implicates the interests of the state in maintaining law and order while guaranteeing fundamental rights of competent representation and a fair trial to those accused of wrongdoing.

This chapter explores the primary divisions of criminal law practice. The first two sections deal with prosecution and defense practice respectively. The third section on white collar crime addresses the growing field of criminal activity in the corporate and business arena. A final section talks about criminal investigation, a law-related area that some lawyers find preferable to the pressures and uncertainties of trial practice.

PROSECUTION

In every American jurisdiction some individual is charged by law with the responsibility of prosecuting criminal cases on behalf of the sovereign. This person may be the U.S. or state attorney general, U.S. attorney, state's attorney, district attorney, county attorney, or city attorney. Criminal statutes provide which courts have jurisdiction over which cases, and who shall prosecute them. Depending on the size of the political subdivision and the caseload involved, the prosecuting attorney may handle such work on a part-time basis, head a staff of hundreds of lawyers, or anything in between. In larger prosecutors' offices there are several levels of attorneys depending on experience and supervisory responsibility. The lawyers tend to be highly specialized in a single area of prosecution, although new attorneys may rotate through several divisions before finally settling on one. The chief prosecutor may seldom if ever try a case personally. Smaller offices are usually less specialized, and impose greater responsibility on new lawyers at an earlier point in their careers.

Regardless of jurisdiction, the role of prosecuting attorney is similar. The prosecutor's office begins working with the police early in a case. Although in many situations arrest follows closely on the heels of the crime, some criminal activity may be the subject of lengthy investigation. In such cases, a representative of the prosecuting attorney's office may work closely with the police to make sure that witnesses are interviewed, evidence is collected, and theories are explored. This activity can help avoid "getting people off on a technicality," mentioned previously. It can also expedite prosecution once someone is arrested.

Many states use a grand jury system for major crimes. In order to indict someone, the state must present its basic case to the grand jury in a closed setting. The state need not prove its case beyond a reasonable doubt, and a defense attorney will not be present to challenge the prosecutor. If in this setting, however, the state cannot convince the grand jurors of probable guilt of the accused, it may not go forward with a public trial. Whether or not there is a grand jury proceeding, the prosecutor's office must undertake an investigation of the case in preparation for a trial. This will involve continuing to work with police and special investigators.

At some point after the arrest, the prosecutor will begin to deal with defense counsel for the accused. Although many criminal defendants retain counsel, a high percentage are represented by public defenders or other appointed counsel.

The prosecuting attorney and defense attorney usually engage in a process known as plea bargaining. Under this system, the defendant may plead guilty to a lesser charge (e.g., simple assault rather than assault with a deadly weapon) or seek a sentence lesser than the state would seek at trial (e.g., probation). Plea bargaining takes place in part because there is no way the state could try every person accused of a crime without long delays or greatly increased numbers of prosecutors and judges. If the two attorneys and the defendant agree upon a plea, the court may accept the plea and sentence the defendant without an expensive and time-consuming trial. Since in many jurisdictions the majority of cases are disposed through plea bargain, negotiating skills are important for the prosecutor and defense attorney alike.

If the parties cannot reach agreement on a plea, the case will go to trial. A criminal trial involves the presentation of evidence by the state and defense. While the state must prove the defendant's guilt beyond a reasonable doubt, the defense does not have to prove anything. The defendant is not required to testify, and defense strategy may simply be to argue that the state has not proved its case. Although defendants have a constitutional right to a trial by jury, many of them waive a jury trial in favor of trial before the judge. If the defendant is acquitted, he may not be tried again. If, however, he is convicted, the state can expect a variety of appeals. The prosecutor's office must continue to represent the state in these appeals by opposing such motions in an appellate court.

Concerning the work of prosecuting attorneys, most of the cases are less than glamorous. Witnesses for accused criminals are sometimes unsavory themselves. Victims may not always be cooperative. The resources to fully investigate many crimes may be missing. Constant contact with the criminal justice system can breed cynicism. As government employees, prosecuting attorneys are not highly paid. Why would one pursue such a career? Many young lawyers believe that work in a prosecutor's office is the best preparation for trial practice that there is. Many genuinely believe that they are doing something necessary and good for society. Some view the prosecutor's high visibility as an entrée to political office. Although some lawyers stay in criminal prosecution throughout their careers, others move into private practice or other parts of the government sector.

CRIMINAL DEFENSE

Opposing the prosecutor in court is the criminal defense attorney. This area of practice is highly litigation-oriented. There is very little preventive criminal practice (lawyers get into trouble when they try to help people to avoid prosecution for criminal activities!). Criminal defense lawyers include both public defenders and private practitioners. Public defenders are appointed by the state to represent individuals accused of crimes who cannot afford to hire a lawyer. Probably the majority of public defenders work for legal aid or a separately funded government agency. In some jurisdictions, court-appointed private practitioners handle the public defender function, and in some small towns the job of public defender may be a part-time one. Retained attorneys represent accused who can afford to hire counsel. The question of whether an accused indigent gets the same quality of representation as someone with a deep pocketbook is a perplexing one, beyond the scope of this book. Whether appointed or retained, the defense attorney owes special loyalty to the accused to assure that constitutional safeguards are not infringed, to present the best possible defense, and to require the state to prove its case beyond a reasonable doubt. The role of defense counsel is often misunderstood by the public. The defense lawyer is not required to agree with the defendant or even to believe that the defendant is blameless. The lawyer is, in fact, ethically prohibited from assisting in the furtherance of criminal activity of the client. This does not prevent the defense lawyer from presenting the best case possible or from putting the state to its proof.

Many lawyers are very uncomfortable with criminal defense work and will avoid it at almost any cost. Others find the work challenging and exciting. Among lawyers in private practice, a fairly small number handle criminal cases exclusively. Many practice criminal law in combination with some form of civil litigation. Because criminal defendants are individuals, and the lawyer-client relationship tends to be one-on-one, a disproportionate number of criminal lawyers are also solo practitioners. There are no large firms with an exclusive or predominant criminal practice. As a final note, criminal law practice is often one of the least remunerative areas. Although a very small percentage of criminal lawyers can demand seemingly exorbitant fees, the average criminal lawyer cannot expect to become wealthy from the practice of law.

WHITE COLLAR CRIME

In recent years, a number of statutes have imposed criminal penalties upon businesses for their actions. Traditional crimes such as fraud and embezzlement have proliferated in our high-tech corporate environment. Some statutes (e.g., RICO), aimed originally at organized crime, have been utilized to prosecute other forms of corporate criminal activity. All these developments have contributed to the recognition of a new subspecialty in criminal law involving white collar crime. Some prosecutors' offices have set up special white collar crime units. A number of corporations have included lawyers with knowledge of criminal law in their corporate law departments. Outside, a subspecialty of practitioners who focus on these business-related crimes has appeared.

Most people do not think about corporations when they consider criminal law. They see muggers, murderers, and rapists. Today, however, the defendant may be Exxon for spilling oil in Prince William Sound. Or it may be a bank vice president who helps launder drug money. Or it may be a graduate student who breaks into the nation's defense computer system. As technology advances and a larger percentage of the country's jobs are classified as white collar, the incidence of white collar crime will probably increase. It follows that this area of practice will grow as well in the coming decades.

CRIMINAL INVESTIGATION

Although the majority of private investigators are not lawyers, some lawyers enjoy the research and investigative side of criminal practice more than trying cases. These lawyers sometimes make careers in investigative work. Interestingly, one of the best known and highly respected investigation agencies in the world is the Federal Bureau of Investigation. For years the FBI has recruited its special agents heavily from the ranks of law school graduates (Even J. Edgar Hoover was a lawyer.). A small percentage of employees of many other law enforcement agencies are lawyers as well. Although it is not uncommon for police officers to go to law school and later enter private practice, some individuals never leave law enforcement and others enter law enforcement after going to law school.

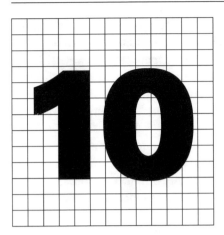

ELDER LAW

During the 1990s, a new term increasingly became fashionable within the ranks of legal practitioners. That term is *elder law* and it refers to the legal representation of individuals who are older members of society. Although there is no fixed date at which a person becomes "old" (retirement age in many companies is 65 or 70; membership in the American Association of Retired Persons—AARP—is available to individuals 55 or older), there is a rough sense that sometime during this period people cross the threshold from being middle-aged to elderly.

People reach a time in life where their children have grown up and moved away (the so-called "empty-nesters") and they can think about more leisure time, retirement, and baby-sitting grandchildren. They are likely to face an increasing number of health-related problems as the years pass. They are likely to contemplate the necessity of disposing of their worldly possessions after they die. It should not be surprising, then, that the legal concerns of older citizens would be different from those of younger people.

Three specific factors contribute to the rise of elder law issues today. First, actuarially, people are living longer now than ever before. Advances in medical science, changes in eating habits and lifestyles, and economic prosperity have all combined to push life expectancies in the United States well into the seventies. In fact, someone who has survived the mortality risks of childhood and youth can expect to live well beyond eighty. Second, the baby boomers are getting old. The same post-World War II bulge in population that swelled the elementary schools in the 1950s, graduate schools in the 1970s, and the workforce through the 1980s will swell the ranks of older citizens for the first part of the twenty-first century. Third, these relatively healthy aging baby boomers are predicted to lead lifestyles very different from those of their own grandparents. They will have leisure time and money to spend. When they have problems, whether medical or political, they will be proactive in forging solutions. They will, as they always have, turn to the law as a vehicle for establishing and protecting their rights.

Elder law is a field that is defined by the clientele rather than the substantive legal problems. In fact, the field is more of an umbrella for other types of substantive practice that are commonly provided for older clients. It is a buzzword to describe the legal services that elder citizens are likely to require, including:

Estate Planning—Older individuals contemplating the end of life often seek legal assistance in developing a plan for disposing of their estates. This can be done through a will during the life of the individual. See Chapter 18 for more information on estate planning.

Health Law—The fact that older people are statistically more likely to experience health problems means that more of them will have contact with the health care system. As that system changes, and to the extent that lawyers are involved in representing people with health care problems, health law issues will be a major component of elder law. See Chapter 13 for more information on health law.

Real Estate—Many retired people at some point sell the homes they have lived in and move to retirement communities, small homes, condos, or health care facilities. Thus, there is a high probability that older people will have one or more experiences with real estate law. For more information on this topic, see Chapter 18.

Social Security—At age 65, most individuals become eligible for Social Security, Medicare, and other government benefits. As with any government system, many people encounter problems getting the right benefits in a timely fashion. Frequently, they require legal assistance. Issues related to Medicare and Medicaid are covered in more detail in Chapter 13.

Pensions and Retirement—A variety of legal problems are associated with the process of retirement itself. The terms of companies' retirement policies are not always clear. The timing of retirement is not always agreed upon by employees and their employers. The value of a departing business owner's equity in the business or succession to leadership is not always clear. The right to and control over pension plan assets and benefits may be ambiguous or confusing. These and other issues frequently end up in the hands of lawyers or the courts.

Other Issues—The elderly face all of the other legal problems that can be found in society. Sometimes age is a factor in the way those problems are handled. Often the personality of the lawyer—being able to communicate with and relate to older people—is significant. The old as well as the young need to feel that they can trust their lawyers.

In one sense, the denomination elder law is shorthand for saying that a firm or individual lawyer concentrates in or is particularly sensitive to older people and their specific legal needs. Anyone practicing law over the next two decades is likely to encounter elderly clients. Regardless of whether it is a minor or major aspect of a person's practice, elder law issues will continue to be an important part of law practice in the United States.

ENVIRONMENTAL LAW

Not too many years ago, environmental law would have been a footnote in the public interest or boutique section of this book. Law schools, if they taught environmental law at all, offered a single esoteric elective that appealed more to the militant environmentalists in Greenpeace than it did to the average law student. Environmental practice was the domain of a few public interest organizations that believed environmental policies could be affected through legal action. Environmental law was anything but mainstream.

Times have changed. A growing awareness that environmental problems are pervasive and global has catapulted this area of law into prominence as a practice area. The federal Environmental Protection Agency has become established as the preeminent watchdog agency for environmental affairs. Many analogous state environmental agencies contribute to a growing enforcement effort under various environmental protection statutes. At the same time, citizen suits either by individuals or public interest organizations have become increasingly recognized as "private attorneys general." Between these government and private initiatives, environmental law emerged as a subject area that cuts across a large number of other legal transactions, and a specialty that requires technical as well as legal knowledge. Over the years, environmental law has developed to the point where it may be called one of the major categories of law practice today and for the foreseeable future.

This chapter is divided into several sections. The first deals with early efforts at *environmental regulation* through the action known as *nuisance*. The second section addresses questions involving the network of laws that has evolved in the environmental field. The third deals with natural resources law and the related subject of *energy.* The fourth section talks about *toxic torts,* a variation of product liability law. A fifth section deals with *land use planning.*

The practice of environmental law implicates a number of other substantive areas including property, torts, administrative law, and litigation. Environmental lawyers work for the government, private associations, law firms, and corporations. They frequently possess advanced technical and scientific degrees in addition to a J.D. Increasingly, they take three to six courses or more in law school or obtain an advanced legal degree to prepare them for this highly technical and specialized field of practice. If the proliferation of law school courses, programs, journals, and articles on environmental law is any indication, this specialty will continue to grow. At the same time, it is clear that environmental law is not an area for generalists. A J.D. and a desire to clean up the world is not enough.

Environmental law is frequently multinational; because environmental problems such as acid rain or nuclear meltdowns do not know geographic boundaries, environmental practice will be international in character. At the same time, environmental law is often local law, local landowners and businesses dealing with local governments to use land in a way that has implications for neighbors and the community at large.

Funding for environmental protection activities is limited. Even in the federal government, cutbacks have limited what the EPA can do. Most of the money for jobs in environmental law remains in the hands of the companies and individuals who are being sued. Some may think it anomalous to say that a lawyer working for a major polluter practices environmental law but this is in fact the case. As in other areas of the law, such as criminal prosecution and defense, plaintiff personal injury work and insurance defense, landlord-tenant law, and labor-management relations, there are two distinct sides to environmental representation. This does not mean that all companies are bad, or that all citizens groups are good, merely that those who enter the field of environmental law must make choices about who they will represent. It also seems at this time that it is possible to move from one side of the docket to the other, or in and out of government practice. The lines are not as rigid as they have become in an area like labor law. Whether this remains the case in the future is hard to tell.

NUISANCE, TRESPASS, AND STRICT LIABILITY

There are many precursors to present-day environmental law, including cases involving poaching the King's deer, and maintaining a manmade pond on land where water escapes through a mine shaft and damages the property of others. These older cases often relied on one of three theories: nuisance, trespass, or strict liability. Nuisance is an action for the loss of use and enjoyment of land due to the conduct of others outside the property. A nuisance may involve any activity such as polluting the water or air, which diminishes an owner's enjoyment of his land. An action for trespass is the proper remedy for physical invasion of the owner's property, as when a miner's sludge slides down the mountainside and onto someone's property. As science has advanced, the technical line between whether or not there is a physical invasion has changed. For instance, we now know that airborne pollution can produce residues of contaminants that remain on the land. In strict liability, one who engages in an abnormally dangerous activity such as blasting, maintaining wild animals, or damming water may be liable for the consequences of those activities without regard to fault.

Over the years, these disparate theories coalesced into modern environmental law. Although the older actions were often utilized in economic disputes between landowners, they became the weapons of choice for environmentalists seeking to stop polluters. The nuisance action particularly proved effective because the plaintiff could ask for an injunction to stop the pollution. Despite the success of individual lawsuits, environmental pollution proved to be a larger problem than could be solved exclusively through civil lawsuits, which attacked environmental contamination after it had occurred rather than preventing it.

A NETWORK OF LAWS

In order to get to the root of pollution, environmentalists have lobbied to change environmental policy at both the national and state levels. They have succeeded in many instances in securing the passage of laws that affect the environment (e.g., federal emissions controls for automobiles). Laws now mandate the cleanup of hazardous waste sites. Laws require developers to file environmental impact statements before proceeding with their plans. These laws cut into every corner of the business world. It is safe to say that no enterprise affecting the environment today can operate without contemplating the pervasive web of laws and regulations dealing with environmental issues.

The creation of enforcement agencies at all levels of the government with the power to promulgate regulations, issue licenses and permits, and penalize wrongdoers has become widespread. Today, environmental attorneys are not simply a small band of do-gooders, filing occasional nuisance suits to stop the most egregious polluters. Lawyers are involved in government at the policy-making and enforcement levels. They work in business and industry, not simply to help their clients avoid the environmental laws, but to advise their clients how to meet their business objectives within the bounds of the law. While some would agree that environmental regulations bog down business development in a morass of detail, others would argue that in order to save the planet, present efforts have not gone far enough. In this sense the debate over the environment is not finished, and lawyers on both sides of the issue are involved in legislative and lobbying work setting the agenda for the next century.

EDUCATION

Part of the environmental agenda falls in the educational sphere. Through formal schooling, public education, and political debate, all people have become sensitized to environmental problems. Many environmental groups continue to try to inform people and businesses about important issues. At another level, education involves research. Many products that were originally considered harmless have been discovered through research to be toxic. Although lawyers usually leave the experimental testing to scientists, lawyers utilize the results of such research in lawsuits, administrative hearings, and other situations where they represent their clients. Knowledge of scientific methods and specific fields of scientific research may be not only useful but necessary for some environmental lawyers. Likewise, an understanding of administrative law and the regulatory process is critical to success in many facets of environmental law, and lawyers who practice in this area must develop these critical skills.

NATURAL RESOURCES AND ENERGY LAW

As a nation that runs on energy, Americans are dependent on power sources that affect the environment. Regardless of the type of power—hydroelectric, coal, oil, nuclear, or solar—environmental consequences flow from their use. From oil spills to nuclear meltdowns to urban emissions from automobiles, energy law cannot escape its link to environmental law. This was not always so. Oil and gas law, mining law, and other areas affecting energy production originally involved the rights of landowners, miners or drillers, producers, and distributors of energy products. Energy policy involves serious questions such as the depletion of nonrenewable energy sources and the cost-effectiveness of alternative forms of energy. Energy law also involves problems in transporting products to consumers by rail, tanker, pipeline, or wire. Again, the rights and responsibilities of those involved in (and those who come in contact with) this distribution system produce complex legal questions. The 1976 oil embargo and the 1991 Gulf War with Iraq point out the intractable global nature of these problems.

Without minimizing the importance of energy problems, it is probably fair to say that energy, from mining to consumption, is a factor in almost every form of environmental pollution. To talk about energy outside of the context of environmental law would be a mistake.

TOXIC TORTS

One of the newer areas within the field of environmental law has become known as toxic torts. Environmental contamination has the potential to injure not just a few individuals but thousands or millions of people. In one sense, the legal system is totally incapable of resolving problems so big. In another sense, however, the system must find ways to compensate victims who have legal claims. Substances such as DES, asbestos, DDT, and even crude oil have proven their capacity to cause widespread damage. What substances will produce tomorrow's environmental disasters remain to be seen, but if past history is any predictor of the future, the last and possibly not worst of these has yet to be seen.

The field of toxic torts has emerged largely because of the development of product liability law. The basic principle of product liability law was articulated by California Chief Justice Roger Traynor in *Greenman v. Yuba Power Products Inc.*: "The weight of modern law now holds that those who place products into the stream of commerce are strictly liable to the ultimate users of those products for damages." This means that someone who is injured by a product need not show that the manufacturer was intentionally wrongful or even negligent in its production methods. By manufacturing and distributing the product, the manufacturer becomes responsible for the injuries it causes, on the theory that the producer is in a better position than the consumer to bear the loss because it can spread the cost of the loss to all purchasers of the product and in may cases insure against the risk. By placing this burden on manufacturers, the law seeks to provide an incentive to produce safe products. In practical terms, a suit based upon strict liability is usually easier to prove than one based on negligence. In any event, the advancement of product liability law provided an opportunity for toxic torts litigation to be successful. Because losses from toxic torts tend to be large, expensive, and protracted, litigation is involved. This kind of legal work requires a high degree of expertise.

Another aspect of toxic torts litigation is the effort in some cases to develop alternative mechanisms for dispute resolution. Some cases involve the establishment of ad hoc law firms, created for the purpose of consolidating all claims into one law suit. Some cases have articulated creative theories such as enterprise liability, holding all manufacturers of a particular product (e.g., a drug such as DES) responsible to injured plaintiffs in proportion to their market share of production. In the area of asbestosis where there are millions of claims against manufacturers (some of whom have gone bankrupt as a result), manufacturers have attempted to establish special payment funds and centers for dispute resolution. All these developments involve radical innovations in the legal system and exciting challenges for the lawyers involved.

LAND USE PLANNING

A final area in which environmental law has become a major factor is land use planning. Landowners, buyers, sellers, and developers must all be aware of limitations on their utilization of property. No longer can anyone use and enjoy his or her property without regard for anyone else. Whether it involves the cleanup of hazardous waste left by a prior owner or restrictions on the present use of the property, landowners cannot escape environmental considerations. In this sense, every real property lawyer must also be an environmental lawyer.

Land use planning involves decisions about how land use should be allocated within a larger community. At one level this may involve strict zoning ordinances to limit or control building. At another level it may involve community and regional planning agencies that develop plans for entire counties or states. At another level it may involve regulations involving wetlands, rivers and bays, fragile environmental areas, wildlife habitats, and severance of renewable resources (e.g., lumbering, fishing, farming, and ranching). The task of developing a viable national land use policy that protects the environment and maintains traditional prerogatives and rights of landowners is a formidable one.

FAMILY LAW

The term family law, as used in this book, refers both to *domestic relations* and *juvenile law*. Among practitioners the terms family law and domestic relations are frequently used interchangeably. Thus, this organization represents a departure from usual classifications. Juvenile law represents a natural subgroup within family law. Taken together, these areas cover legal problems of people living together in family units. As American society has grown more complex and the traditional nuclear family has disintegrated to some degree, new structures are evolving for which some of the older rules do not seem to apply. The legal needs of certain groups within the family (e.g., battered spouses) are also attracting attention.

DOMESTIC RELATIONS

Domestic relations has always been a fundamental area of law practice. People in every community get married, have children, and sometimes get divorced. Few private practitioners will escape having some contact with domestic relations matters. For many general practice firms domestic relations constitutes a significant part of its bread and butter practice. In small towns, particularly, where lawyers tend to represent families and individuals over a long period of time, domestic relations is a natural part of the practice. Unlike many areas of law practice, there have long been specialists in domestic relations. Some, like Marvin Mitchelson and Raul Felder, have developed national reputations for their work. Many other specialists in domestic relations work tirelessly for their clients without such publicity.

The heart of domestic relations practice is divorce. Statistics tell the story: 40 percent of all marriages will end in divorce. In most of these divorces the parties are represented by at least one and usually two lawyers. This is because divorce is the quintessential adversarial process. It is very difficult for one lawyer to represent the differing interests of two hostile parties, although many would argue that an uncontested divorce, where the terms of the separation are not disputed, can be handled by a single lawyer to reduce costs (the term that is sometimes used, "amicable divorce," is probably an oxymoron).

Divorce work may involve a number of different aspects. One of the first is counseling. Because of the emotionally charged setting, the high degree of stress most clients feel, and the personal nature of the lawyer–client relationship, this is one area of law where active listening, interpersonal skills, and other counseling skills are critical. It is virtually impossible to separate the client's legal problems from personal ones. These pressures place special demands on the domestic relations lawyer. First, most lawyers are not trained as professional counselors although they use counseling skills on a regular basis. A few lawyers may be certified counselors, but those who are not often find it necessary to refer the client to a qualified psychotherapist or psychiatrist. Other referrals to community-based agencies (e.g., a battered women center) may be necessary from time to time. Knowing when and how to utilize such support services can be invaluable to the representation of a client in crisis. Since an important objective of the domestic relations laws is the maintenance of the family, part of the counseling process may involve seeking reconciliation. Unfortunately, the adversary process sometimes undermines efforts to save the marriage. A good divorce lawyer should be sensitive to this possibility.

Another real danger in an area where clients frequently feel rejected and lawyers act as caring helpers is that personal feelings can get out of hand. The problem of sexual relations with clients is a very sensitive one, and states such as California and New York have passed regulations prohibiting sexual relationships with clients. Certainly, sex between consenting adults is widely accepted in many quarters these days; but the problems inherent in such relationships between lawyers and their clients (particularly in divorce cases) far outweigh the benefits.

Another aspect of divorce work is negotiation. Either or both of two bones of contention are involved in most contested divorces: property settlement and child custody. Property and custody disputes can be extremely acrimonious and the lawyer may be hampered by parties who do not foster a peaceful resolution of the conflict.

The divorce lawyer must also be skilled at drafting legal documents. These documents include not only court papers but also separation agreements reached by way of the negotiation process. If parties can reach agreement on the settlement of property, custody, and visitation claims, they may be able to avoid a bitter and expensive trial. If it comes to that, however, a divorce lawyer must be a competent trial lawyer.

Matrimonial law can also be practiced preventively. Many couples today negotiate prenuptial agreements establishing property and custody rights at a time when the parties are on speaking terms.

In the 1990s, nontraditional families are becoming the norm. Unmarried cohabitants, same-sex couples, second marriages with mixed families, adoptive families, and other living arrangements have become more prevalent. Domestic relations lawyers today are more likely than ever to encounter these nontraditional families. Additionally, the demise of intrafamily immunity (prohibiting suits by family members against each other) has opened the door to various family torts that did not exist in the past (e.g., spousal battery).

JUVENILE LAW

Juvenile law is a branch of family law that deals specifically with children. Sometimes children are overlooked in disputes between parents. Their views and rights in matters such as visitation and support are sometimes disregarded. Juvenile law focuses directly on the rights of the children, irrespective of the problems of their parents. This may involve appointing separate counsel for children in a marital dispute, appointing a guardian, naming a trustee for funds to support the children, or even protecting the children from abuse. All of these matters generally come under the jurisdiction of a distinct family court system. Juvenile law may involve questions of shelter, foster care, education, nourishment, and health. The court acting in the best interest of the child may sometimes terminate the normal parental authority. For example, parents who belong to a religious group that refuses medical treatment sometimes end up in conflict with the family court over the best interests of their sick children. Most states have agencies whose purpose is specifically the protection of children, and these agencies must be represented by counsel. In addition, since many of these children are poor, welfare agencies and legal aid offices handle an inordinate amount of juvenile law.

A separate facet of juvenile law involves problem children. These children may have learning disabilities such as dyslexia or low IQs; behavioral problems, such as autism or hyperactivity; or debilitating health problems. In all these areas, there are sensitive issues involving decisions about treatment, hospitalization, or institutionalization. The stigma associated with therapeutic treatment can be devastating to young lives. Without treatment, however, some children will grow up to become dysfunctional adolescents and adults.

For juveniles who exhibit antisocial behavior, whether related to childhood disabilities or not, a juvenile court system remains as a last resort. Although juvenile courts in theory are not criminal courts, the conduct they adjudicate is very similar to that encountered in the criminal courts for adults. In recent years, an increasing number of jurisdictions permit juveniles to be tried as adults under certain circumstances. Whereas the power of the juvenile court to incarcerate individuals ends at the age of majority, for persons whose crimes are serious enough, imprisonment beyond the age of eighteen may be desirable.

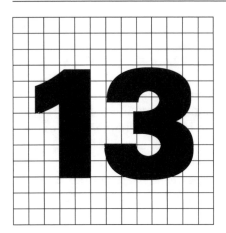

HEALTH LAW

The burgeoning field of health law has become increasingly important as changes in medical and health care systems have permeated society. In former times, medicine was a fairly simple business; people went to a family doctor for routine ailments or to a local hospital for more serious procedures for most of their medical treatments. The dentist, too, was a local practitioner who handled all but the most complex cases. People lived as best they could until disease or injury cut them down.

The twentieth century and particularly the mechanized warfare of two world wars and subsequent conflicts ushered in radical therapies for combating serious trauma, disease, and mental disorders. Medical science replaced home remedies as a way to fight an increasing variety of maladies. Hospitals became research and teaching hospitals, no longer just places to go to wait for a recovery from surgery. As the volume of medical knowledge advanced, doctors and other health professionals found it necessary to specialize in narrow fields of practice. Allied professions such as psychotherapy, rehabilitation, laboratory testing, and others grew up in support of primary medical services. In the workplace, medical insurance became a common method of covering medical costs, particularly the enormous expenses associated with catastrophic major medical situations.

Over the years the cost of health services escalated consistently to cover the cost of this increasingly complex system. Medical malpractice lawsuits and government regulations added to these costs as protection against the risk of liability were as passed on to consumers. In order to manage the spiraling costs of health care, the insurance industry struggled to identify alternative managed care systems such as health maintenance organizations (HMOs). Congress has engaged periodically in a national health care debate, which continues.

All of this suggests that this isn't your grandfather's health care system anymore. What should be clear in this end-of-the-century era is that health care permeates our lives. People today utilize a variety of health care professionals in a diversity of approaches, many of which were unheard of even a generation ago. Significantly, there has been a major shift for both patients and professionals away from treatment toward prevention. Diet, exercise, and mental health are examples of ways people today reduce the risks of health care problems.

This trend in turn interacts with two other phenomena. The first may be described as patient autonomy: the right of a patient to make decisions about what to do with his or her body. This concept differs from the paternalistic model of traditional medicine in which patients deferred to the informed judgment of their doctors. Patients today want more information and want to make more decisions about their prevention and treatment alternatives.

The second phenomenon is that people are actually living longer. Actuarial tables demonstrate that life expectancies today are longer than for any period in history. Old people today are in their eighties, not in their sixties or forties as in some more primitive civilizations. Demographically, there are more older people in society (See Chapter 10 on Elder Law.). In our time, some diseases have been virtually eliminated while others that were unheard of in the past have emerged to become major health problems.

It should come as no surprise that such a massive industry as health care should produce a host of attendant legal problems, or that such problems often require the services of lawyers to address them. Although lawyers are not well-regarded in some quarters of the health field, it is almost impossible to imagine so many diverse rights and interests being protected without lawyers, as if one could click her heels three times and the health care crisis would evaporate and society could return to those bygone days when everyone had a friendly family physician who made house calls.

The chapter will examine some of the work that lawyers perform in the health care field. As with many other specialties, such as taxation, health law can be divided between specialists who devote a substantial part of their time to health care issues and to other lawyers who inevitably encounter health care problems in the course of their particular work. Health care lawyers work in a variety of settings, including private firms, corporations, government agencies, and not-for-profit associations.

MALPRACTICE

No discussion of health law would be complete without mentioning medical malpractice (See also Chapter 21 on tort law.). Simply put, doctors are required to exercise the same degree of skill as a doctor of ordinary prudence in their treatment of patients. Doctors are also required to provide patients with sufficient information about treatment alternatives to allow the patients to make informed choices about such treatment. When doctors make mistakes, individuals are harmed, patients die, and treatments don't work. It is not the case that doctors are required to successfully cure their sick patients, only to apply their skill and knowledge with ordinary professional prudence. If the doctor fails to do so and causes injury to the patient, the patient has a right to recover for those injuries. Although recovery in a malpractice action cannot undo what has been done, it can compensate the victim for his loss and, in appropriate circumstances, punish the wrongdoer for gross mistakes.

Health professionals are almost always protected by malpractice insurance, the premiums for which can be extremely expensive. What doctor in her right mind, however, would not protect against the prospect of a legal liability by procuring insurance against the potential risk of being sued?

Lawyers represent both plaintiffs/patients and doctors/defendants. They may also work directly for the insurance company in protecting the companies' interests. Although malpractice defense work tends to be concentrated in a fairly small number of larger defense-oriented law firms, plaintiffs' lawyers are more likely to be small firm lawyers or solo practitioners.

DOCTORS, HOSPITALS, AND HMOS

As the relationships between care providers and institutions has grown more complex, lawyers have been called upon increasingly to represent the parties in contract negotiations. For instance, an HMO will require a participating doctor to sign an agreement with the HMO as a condition of participating in the panel. The details of such relationships are often hammered out between the lawyers for the opposing sides of the transactions. Lawyers for hospitals may represent the institution on a variety of other matters, including contracts with vendors and suppliers, construction, labor relations, non-malpractice liability (e.g., such as when a visitor to the hospital slips and falls on a wet floor). Lawyers representing doctors often find themselves handling other types of transactions for their clients, including real estate transactions, family law, estate planning, and representation in nonmedical businesses.

LEGAL–MEDICAL ETHICS

Many of the problems in health care raise serious moral, philosophical, and ethical issues. The decisions we make about these questions are not just intellectual exercises. They determine who lives and who dies, who gets treatment and who does not, who pays and who goes free. It is far beyond the scope of this book to discuss these ethical issues, but some of them are listed here: When does a patient have a right to die? Who decides to cut off life-support systems for chronically or terminally ill patients? Should individuals have the right to end their lives if they are suffering from terminal illnesses? Should health care professionals be required to or allowed to assist patients in their efforts to take their own lives? Do unborn children have any right to recover for injuries inflicted upon them prior to birth? Is the ultimate fetal injury, abortion, a right of the mother to decide what to do with her body or is it murder? At what age can children make decisions for themselves about medical treatment? In what situations can adults lose their capacity to make medical decisions for themselves? When that happens, who decides for them: their families or their doctors? Should society spend the money to find a cure for AIDS or should it spend the money on better methodologies for plastic surgery? What is insanity, and when should it excuse individuals from the consequences of tortious or criminal conduct? The list could go on and on.

In all of these situations the term medical–legal ethics is applied because the issues have both medical and legal implications. Neither doctors nor lawyers alone can address the nuances of such issues, but just browsing through almost any newspaper makes clear that these issues are common; scarcely a day goes by that some story or other does not address one of these issues or some other like it.

HEALTH AND ENVIRONMENT

In many ways health law intersects with environmental law and toxic torts. Where pollutants are emitted into the atmosphere or discharged into waterways; where wastes are buried underground or dumped at sea; where chemical substances are stored or transported; where crops are treated with pesticides or buildings insulated with harmful artificial substances, serious health problems arise. Maybe housing developments have been built on toxic waste dumps. Perhaps pollutants may leach into public water supplies. Or maybe oil tankers break apart on heavy seas, or nuclear radiation escapes into the atmosphere when a nuclear reactor core melts down. Such mass disasters may harm thousands or even millions of individuals. The injuries may not manifest themselves for months, or years, or decades after contact with the toxic substances. When health problems begin to emerge, the original manufacturers of the toxins may not even be in business. Liability in such actions may literally bring down an entire industry, as in the case of asbestosis and asbestos.

PUBLIC POLICY

The parameters of the public policy debate on health care are significant at all levels of the government. In the legislative halls, political action committees, citizens groups, research institutions, and think tanks, the future of the health care system is discussed and reviewed. Many of the people involved in this process are lawyers. Lawyers serve not only as legislators but as administrative officials, aides, and representatives of proponents in various public forums. Lawyers may be found actively involved in the drafting of legislation and regulations. In short, as long as the public policy debate on health care continues, lawyers will have an opportunity to participate in molding that policy.

IMMIGRATION LAW

Throughout its history, the United States has welcomed immigrants from other lands. New arrivals to this country were attracted by political and religious freedom, economic opportunity, and the prospect of a new start in a new land. Throughout the nineteenth and early twentieth centuries, millions of immigrants came to the United States through Ellis Island in New York Harbor. Since World War II, American immigration policies have become much stricter, but the influx of people from different parts of the world has not waned.

In recent decades, immigrants have come to the United States from Central and Eastern Europe, from the Far East including large numbers of Vietnamese after the war, from the Indian sub-continent, from Africa, from Central and South America, and from the Caribbean. By far the largest number of immigrants have come from Mexico, as workers migrated to find employment outside of their homeland. Not only did the United States offer a promise of jobs but also an infrastructure of American Spanish-speakers throughout the southwest. Today there are Latino communities in virtually every major city in the United States as well as most rural farming and ranching areas.

A common thread among all of these immigrant groups is that they often need legal services yet lack access to existing legal institutions. Many newcomers face language barriers in an English-speaking legal system. Others may come from oppressive political systems where lawyers' and judges' primary loyalty was to the state, or where corruption permeated society. Still others came from cultures where problems were typically resolved privately rather than institutionally. All came from nations where the substantive laws differed in some respects with those of their new home. And all had to deal at some time in some way with their legal status in this country.

The most visible aspect of immigration law involves questions of legal entry into the United States. Foreign nationals can gain entry for a variety of different reasons including work, marriage, and political asylum. The process of obtaining necessary legal documentation to remain in the United States often involves the assistance of a lawyer. In many cases the person's initial entry into the United States was not legal, complicating the lawyer's task. Immigration lawyers may also be involved in opposing efforts to deport aliens who have not secured proper legal status to remain in the United States.

The immigration part of immigration law is the tip of the iceberg. Because immigrants have legal problems just like everyone else, they generate a substantial amount of regular legal work. Additionally, because they lack contacts with traditional law firms, they are likely to continue to use lawyers who specialize in immigration law for other forms of legal representation. Immigrants may have legal problems dealing with housing, education, health care, family matters, personal injuries, labor and employment issues, and the police. Because of the language barriers, fluency of the language of the immigrant is often critical to effective representation of individuals in the group; many immigrants who speak a common language such as Spanish come from different countries with different cultures. These people value lawyers who possess knowledge and understanding of their particular customs.

Since many immigrants are poor, they may qualify for a variety of public assistance programs, including representation through legal aid and public defender programs. In recent years there has been public debate about the extent of benefits that undocumented aliens should receive. Denial of government benefits is more likely to change the forum in which immigrants' legal issues are decided than to eliminate the underlying legal issues themselves. Whether or not a government health benefit program pays for treatment or not will have no effect on whether someone gets sick.

It is probable that the millions of current immigrants to the United States will continue to require legal services for a generation or more, until their children become assimilated into American society. If history is any indicator, it is likely that new waves of immigrants will come to this country as long as conditions here are perceived as better than they are in other parts of the world. As long as these situations continue to exist, immigration law will be a vital and robust area of practice.

INTELLECTUAL PROPERTY LAW

The area of intellectual property law is not a new one. The Anglo-American legal system has long recognized that not all property interests are embodied in a tangible form. Real property can be seen and measured; personal property in the form of physical objects can be seen and touched. Other property interests, however, are intangible, such as ownership of a company, which may be represented by a stock certificate but which is essentially nonphysical. Intellectual property falls into this last category of intangible assets. It has the further attribute of having been created through the intellectual efforts of the writer, inventor, or artist.

The law makes a simple assumption about most intellectual property: the creator ought to have the right to exploit or to refrain from exploiting the fruits of her labor. Just as ownership of land carries with it rights to determine who may come onto the land and when, intellectual property rights give the possessor the right to decide who can have access to the intellectual property and under what circumstances.

The law is further complicated by the assumption that an idea itself cannot be protected, but only the particular process or embodiment of that idea. For instance, the idea of an obsessed sea captain on a maniacal quest to confront and destroy a whale that had caused the loss of his leg cannot itself be protected. But if a guy named Melville told the story in his own words about a captain named Ahab, a ship called the Pequod, a mariner named Ishmael, and a great white whale named Moby Dick, then Melville ought to be paid for the distribution of his version of the story. The intellectual property is the organization, choice of words, and detail that the author brings to the work.

Intellectual property law can be divided into five main categories: copyrights, patents, trademarks, trade secrets, and moral rights. These will be discussed in the following sections. It is worth noting that the field of intellectual property law has undergone significant growth in recent years with the development of computers and other forms of electronic technology. New machines and new forms of information storage and retrieval have taxed the legal concepts devised in an era of printing presses and the mechanical industrial machinery. Some of the most interesting litigation in the courts today involves defining intellectual property concepts that protect authors, inventors, and artists in today's technological environment. (See Chapter 8, Computer Law, for more information.)

COPYRIGHTS

Copyright law protects authors and publishers from the unauthorized distribution of their work to others. The common law has always recognized the right of an author of any writing to control the dissemination of that work. This applies to everything from letters to manuscripts. Most of copyright law, however, deals with the commercial distribution of books and periodicals. In order to profitably distribute a printed product to a mass market, it is normally necessary to involve a publisher in the development, production, and marketing of an author's work. Although it is possible for authors to self-publish their works, it is very difficult to do so profitably. What most authors do instead is to sell the rights to the distribution of their work to a publisher in return for a royalty or other payment. The author contractually conveys his legal interest in the work to the publisher in return for such payment.

In the United States, copyright law has been modified by federal statute governing many kinds of copyright protection for commercially distributed works. Thus, when a book or magazine is published, in order for the publisher to secure the benefits of the copyright law it must formally register the copyright with the U.S. Copyright Office. The existence of computer databases containing easily accessed and downloaded written works of all sorts makes it much more difficult for publishers and ultimately authors to receive compensation for their efforts.

Lawyers involved in copyright law may represent authors, playwrights, musicians, or others who create distributable products. They may represent people who claim that their intellectual efforts have been stolen or appropriated by others. They may represent publishers, distributors such as bookstores, or anyone else in the chain of product development. Increasingly, lawyers find themselves embroiled in international copyright issues involving American books being distributed abroad, as well as foreign products being imported into this country.

PATENTS

Patent law is a highly specialized field that involves protection for the inventors of machines and other tangible products or processes. The U.S. Patent Office issues patents that give exclusive rights to these developers for the sale or distribution of their inventions. Because the determination of a product's uniqueness is often highly technical and detailed, the process for securing a patent is much more complex than for filing a copyright. This process is so complicated, in fact, that there is a special patent bar (whose members pass a patent bar exam), a special submission process, and even a special court system to govern disputes and appeals. Most patent lawyers work in specialized patent law firms, in patent law departments of large firms, or in specialized divisions of a large corporation. Many other lawyers work on the government side of the patent law system in the Patent Office or Court. Almost all of these lawyers possess an educational background or experience in a technical or scientific field. This is because they are frequently required to utilize their scientific skills as well as legal skills when carrying out their work.

TRADEMARKS

Trademark law deals more with marketing than with product origination. It has long been recognized that name identification is an important element in selling a product. Do you want Coke or Pepsi? Do you drive a BMW or Ford? Do you wear Nikes or Reeboks? This basic marketing rule takes on even greater proportions when products are distributed on a worldwide basis through electronic media to consumers. Visual images, too, can be a part of a product's identity. Think about the Exxon tiger or the golden arches.

Any name or symbol that is exclusively identified with a particular product and used in the marketing of that product can be registered as a trademark and protected against infringement. A trademark owner who fails to assert its trademark may lose its legal interest to the public domain. A product may have become so ubiquitous that its name becomes synonymous with an entire class of products. Xerox Corporation regularly takes out full-page ads in major newspapers and magazines informing people that the copies they make are photocopies, not xeroxes. Coca-Cola takes pains to inform people that not all cola-flavored soft drinks are "Coke." Other problems may include product confusion, such as a Mom and Pop store in New England named after the owners, Bloomingdales, or those Chrysler insignias that look ever so much like a Mercedes Benz logo.

A related area involves the commercial exploitation of an image, as when an entertainer has developed and exploited a unique style and does not want it copied by imitators. One of the more famous cases in this area involved the estate of Bela Lugosi, the actor who created the movie role Dracula.

Many firms that handle copyright cases also handle trademarks. Likewise, many companies that distribute products utilize trademark lawyers in-house. In addition, because of the close relationship between trademarks and marketing, marketing agencies may also be involved in trademark issues. Since a trademark or logo may be designed by a marketing firm, there may even be issues as to who owns the trademark, the marketing agency or the product manufacturer or distributor.

TRADE SECRETS

In today's complex industrial world the process of product design and development is an intensively competitive one. Competing companies may be racing to develop a particular new process or product. Before intellectual property can be patented or otherwise protected, the ongoing research and development efforts generate a work product that enjoys its own protection. Industrial espionage involving the specific invasion of ongoing research, defection of key employees with secret information, and a variety of other issues provide the basis for considerable litigation over these trade secrets. Although much of this trade secret litigation is conducted by law firms that practice in the areas of trademark, copyright, and patent law, it may fall to other films involved in general litigation as well.

MORAL RIGHTS OF ARTISTS

A final category of intellectual property involves what has been called the moral rights of artists. One may create a painting or sculpture or other work of art and may be able to copyright or sell his interest in the work to another. What happens when the successor in interest to a work of art no longer wants it, or wishes to alter it? And what happens if an artist throws away a piece considering it unworthy of his signature and it is picked up by someone else and held out as the genuine thing? Issues such as these go beyond the ordinary scope of copyright law. In Europe, an artist's rights to the integrity of his work has been described as a moral right. The idea of moral rights of artists has been very slow to catch on in the United States. Here, if I should buy the Mona Lisa for display in my living room and decide that she would look better with a moustache, I would be able to paint a moustache on her because I own the painting. If I owned the Sistine Chapel and decided that it needed a new modern whitewashed look without all those musty murals, I might paint it over. No matter what DaVinci or Michelangelo might say (were they alive, of course). No matter what enhanced value the artwork might possess. Increasingly, however, courts are beginning to protect the integrity of artwork in this country. Although the artists may not be able to preclude the sale, distribution, or reproduction of his work, he may be able to prevent its alteration or destruction. Look for this area of intellectual property law to gain increasing prominence in the years ahead.

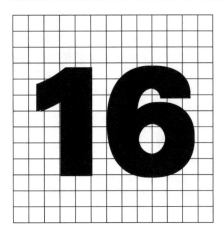

INTERNATIONAL LAW

The field of international law has grown dramatically in recent decades as international relations have become more and more intertwined. Although countries have always had diplomatic relations and engaged in trade, the advent of modern communication and transportation systems has brought the world closer to Marshall McLuhan's notion of a global village. The end of the Cold War and the emergence of the Third World have contributed to the changing international picture. Increasingly, it is becoming clear that some problems such as environmental pollution cannot be solved by single countries alone.

The field of international law can be divided into two broad areas: public international law and private or commercial international law. Although there can be considerable overlap between these two areas, as when governments become involved in trade policies such as tariffs and embargoes, there is a rough separation between the public and private sector. This is more true today than it was during the days of the Cold War, when countries' governments were the alter egos of the economic systems.

PUBLIC INTERNATIONAL LAW

When most people think of international law they think of countries exchanging ambassadors, or the United Nations, or the Nuremberg Trials. From ancient times, nations have maintained diplomatic relations through the exchange of ambassadors. Communications between governments through these ambassadors guided relations between the countries. When diplomatic relations were severed, war, another institution as old as human civilization, often ensued. To be sure, over the centuries nations even developed rules of war and armistice. War constantly redraws the world's political map and changes the balance of power in the international community. There has probably been no time in human history when a state of war did not exist somewhere in the world. Thus, issues of war and peace are intractably interwoven with public international law.

A footnote on this process is the intelligence community. In order to more effectively formulate international policies, governments often seek to gather as much information as they can as to what is going on in other countries. This information gathering can take any form from clandestine espionage to the routine reading of newspapers and other government communications.

The concept of worldwide political organizations took popular form at the end of World War I as the League of Nations. After World War II, the United Nations replaced the League as an international council of government representatives. The United Nations has proliferated numerous international agencies that perform a variety of functions, from a world court to feeding the poor. Over its fifty years of existence, the United Nations has on various occasions engaged in multinational peacekeeping efforts at trouble spots around the globe.

Many people do not realize it but lawyers are often involved in all of the areas described above: diplomatic missions, intelligence work, and international agencies. Legal training provides a solid groundwork for careers in all of these areas, although education or training in international relations, language skills, or political clout may be useful credentials for aspiring public international lawyers. And because the United States exercises considerable influence in the international arena, large numbers of American lawyers are active in this field.

INTERNATIONAL COMMERCIAL LAW

Private international law has evolved gradually over the course of the twentieth century as barriers to trade among nations have diminished. At the same time, multinational corporations that deliver products and services globally have emerged to dominate world trade. International banking now makes the worldwide transfer of funds simple and efficient. Your ATM card works as well in London, or Mexico City, or even Moscow as it does at your corner bank. In this free international market, commerce has proliferated. The European community, the North American Free Trade Agreement, and a general reduction in protective tariffs throughout the world make it increasingly easy for goods to flow across borders. At least some of this commerce has reduced the differences in the availability of products worldwide. Not only do you not have to go to France to buy French wine, but you can also get a Big Mac in Paris.

Private international law is facilitated by commercial transactions negotiated by law firms for their clients. Traditionally, international commercial law was dominated by a few very large firms in New York, London, and other international cities. International trade has grown so much that almost any law firm of any size anywhere in the country can have clients doing business overseas. Whether they are importing or exporting, they still need to work out deals that are legally binding not only in this country but in the other countries where the businesses they deal with are located. Although efforts to create uniform international laws for transactions across borders have met with some degree of success, transnational deals can be exceedingly complex. Even non-legal cultural issues such as how firmly one should shake hands or how close speakers should be when they talk to each other can make or break a deal.

One of the best entrées into international practice remains working for a large law firm with clients who have transnational activities. However, an international practice can develop out of any representation of a client doing business outside of the United States, so international law is no longer limited to a few large firms anymore.

Some people think that international law necessarily means living in or traveling to foreign countries. While there is a good bit of international travel associated with international commercial law, modern communications systems including telephone, fax, overnight document delivery, and the Internet make it easy to practice internationally from offices in the United States, so actual foreign travel is much less than one might expect.

This is an area of practice that is likely to continue to grow in the future. As with other fields of law it will probably be divided between those who are specialists in the area and those who are occasional practitioners. Those who do not practice in the area on a regular basis may need to employ the services of other lawyers who do. And American lawyers working on international commercial problems will find themselves dealing with lawyers from other countries as they perform their services.

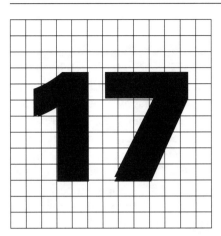

LABOR LAW

The history of labor–management relations in the United States is a fascinating tale. Born out of the Industrial Revolution, nurtured by the vision of manifest destiny in the nineteenth century, and weaned on the New Deal, *labor relations* has developed into a uniquely American body of law. The most significant piece of legislation affecting labor law was the National Labor Relations Act, passed during the Great Depression after decades of bitter, sometimes violent, union-management battles. The Act gave workers the right to bargain collectively with management through elected union representatives for wages and other terms of employment. Circumstances under which a shop could be unionized were spelled out. A delineation of who was labor and who was management was articulated. The rights of all parties in cases involving work stoppages and contract negotiations were defined. In short, the NLRA established ground rules in an area where none had existed.

The legacy of the Act has been the creation of a permanent adversarial relationship between unions and management. This, in turn, has dictated the use of legal representation at every stage of the process. And, not surprisingly, labor lawyers have taken on the colors of their clients. Thus, very few lawyers would even try to represent both labor and management. Today, there are five major groups that deserve mention within the larger field of labor law: union lawyers, management lawyers, government lawyers, arbitrators, and agents. This chapter discusses these groups, along with the related practice area of employment law.

UNION LAWYERS

Union lawyers represent labor unions in contract negotiations, employee grievances, and other dealings with company management. Such lawyers also often represent the union as a business entity, including the management of a sometimes large pension fund. Union lawyers may be retained as in-house counsel for a union or remain as outside counsel in a private law firm. Some union lawyers have developed an ancillary practice representing individual union members on matters outside of the labor–management area. A few unions have created group legal services programs designed to provide such representation for union members. In addition to representing existing unions, union lawyers may represent employees seeking National Labor Relations Board certification as the designated bargaining representative of their company's workers.

MANAGEMENT LAWYERS

Management lawyers represent the company in virtually all matters involving union lawyers. Management lawyers often work in law firms that handle other corporate matters for the company, although they usually work in a separate labor department. Some firms specialize in management-side labor law. Management lawyers often help companies that are not unionized to remain non-union. This may involve working informally with employee groups to meet their needs in such a way that the employees will not feel the need for separate union representation. In those circumstances, however, when the workers begin to organize the National Labor Relations Board carefully monitors the activities of the company and its representatives to assure that employees have the right to organize. At that point the company may become more aggressive in opposing certification of a bargaining representative, and the management legal team will be represented in that effort.

GOVERNMENT LAWYERS

Many labor lawyers got their start practicing at the National Labor Relations Board, the federal agency charged with carrying out the provisions of the National Labor Relations Act. Many other lawyers work for agencies having responsibility over labor-related problems, such as the Equal Employment Opportunity Commission or the Occupational Safety and Health Administration. Other lawyers work for state labor departments. The NLRB is the largest and most important labor agency in the nation. Its roles as a referee in disputes between labor and management and as a rule-making authority give it great power to affect labor-management relations.

ARBITRATION

Labor law has long utilized the mechanism of arbitration to settle disputes nonjudicially. The concept of arbitration is that an independent, fair-minded arbitrator listening to both sides of a dispute can reach a decision that all the parties will accept. Arbitrators come from a variety of walks of life, with a simple common thread that they seldom are identified as either pro-union or pro-management. Most, although not all, are lawyers. They may be former employees of the National Labor Relations Board, former judges, or academics. Many industries have special rules defining when to invoke the arbitration process. In some instances, arbitration has been imposed externally on the disputants. In all cases, however, success of the arbitration process depends upon the willingness of the parties to submit themselves to it. And although the concept of arbitration may be applicable in many different settings, the most notable success for the process has been in the field of labor law.

AGENTS

The subject of agency is discussed in Chapter 22 dealing with sports and entertainment law. It is worth noting here that agents represent individuals or small groups in dealing with management of an organization. Although the agent's client is often an independent contractor rather than an employee, many of the same labor law issues can arise, and the group of athletes, entertainers, or others may be represented by a union as well. Many, although certainly not all agents, handle other work as union-side lawyers.

EMPLOYMENT LAW

Whether it is considered a subset of labor law or a separate field of practice, employment law frequently deals with the same parties as labor law. Employment law problems generally fall outside the framework of the labor law system, and have evolved into distinguishable subspecialties.

Workers Compensation

One of the largest areas of employment law involves workers compensation. During the nineteenth century, work-related injuries to employees caused by machines produced a spate of litigation over employers' liability for such injuries. In many early cases, employers were able to escape liability by pleading one of several defenses available to them under the law. Still, litigation was expensive, and an unfavorable verdict could be crippling, especially to a small business. Over the years, various states passed worker compensation laws that provided an administrative remedy for work-related injuries. These laws typically took the question of fault out of the equation, giving a remedy to a much larger number of injured workers, while fixing the limits of compensation at levels lower than successful plaintiffs might otherwise receive in court. Employers were also required to contribute to a fund for payment of claims. The result was that the cost of work-related injuries was spread across the universe of employers. Additionally, these administrative systems virtually eliminated personal injury litigation for work-related injuries from the court system.

Benefits Law

The broad term *benefits law* encompasses a number of different employee benefits. Modern labor relations has produced a wide range of employee benefits, some negotiated between labor and management, and others established by law. These include health, disability and life insurance, social security, unemployment compensation, pension and retirement plans, and others too numerous to name. Collectively, these benefits implicate a number of other practice areas from labor to tax law to contract law. The common threads are that they involve employees and employers, and that they almost always require lawyers in their construction, application, and interpretation.

EEO

Although the progress of civil rights law has been slow, legislation during the 1960s and 1970s at both national and state levels attempted to deal specifically with the problem of discrimination in the hiring, promotion, and treatment of diverse employees. The Clarence Thomas Supreme Court confirmation hearings demonstrated clearly that equal employment opportunity (EEO) issues have not vanished from the workplace.

At the federal level, the Equal Employment Opportunity Commission handles complaints of discrimination. Many states and some localities also have their own laws governing equal employment, and corresponding agencies to enforce them. As in other areas covered in this book, the existence of a government practice area parallels a private practice area dealing with the same subject. In this case it would be lawyers representing both complainants and employers in administrative hearings and judicial actions. Included in the protection of equal employment laws are racial, ethnic, sexual, veteran, and handicapped minorities; some jurisdictions have also addressed the problems of discrimination based on sexual preference and other nontraditional categories.

Occupational Health and Safety

Occupational health and safety law, sometimes referred to as OSHA law, deals with safety in the workplace. Whereas "workers comp" addresses the problem of workers who are injured, OSHA law attempts to prevent injuries by establishing a safe working environment. Certainly, different industries present different risks of danger; however, OSHA requirements seek to maximize safety and reduce injuries regardless of the work setting. Although many employers decry the intrusiveness of OSHA regulations, the overall effect seems to have been a reduction in work-related injuries due to unsafe conditions.

Americans with Disabilities

The Americans with Disabilities Act (ADA) requires employers to attempt to accommodate qualified individuals who suffer from disabilities. The ADA defines disabilities very broadly, and this has generated substantial legal work and litigation as employers attempt to meet the requirements of the legislation.

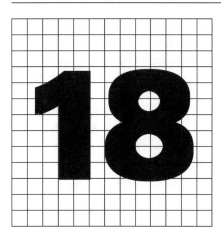

PROPERTY LAW

One of the most basic areas of law practice has always been property law. Property law is generally divided into two main classifications: real property (land) and personal property. In modern times, these broad classifications have splintered into a number of subcategories which will be discussed in this chapter.

A natural corollary of property law is the area of wills and estates, which covers the disposition of property at death. More recently, housing law has developed as an important mechanism for adjudicating the rights and duties of landlords and tenants in this society in which a large number of people rent or lease rather than own their house. The law of leasing, which intersects commercial and business law, has emerged as a mechanism for transferring property for a term so that it can be used by someone other than the ultimate owner. Property law can run the gamut from routine and simple to highly complex and innovative transactions. What is virtually certain is that almost every lawyer will have some dealing with property law, regardless of what the lawyer does or for whom.

REAL PROPERTY

Under the American and English legal systems, land may be owned, transferred, and inherited. This concept that we accept as fundamental does not exist in many other systems. Under feudal systems, all land is ultimately owned by the king or other monarch, and everyone else holds some form of tenancy in the land. Under pure communist systems the state (or the people) own all land and other property. In native American and many other cultures no one could own the land. The particularly Western European concept of land ownership has evolved for over a thousand years into a complex and sometimes arcane set of rules and procedures.

Residential

At the heart of this system a number of ancient documents are used to convey title of property from one person to another. In a simple transaction, a seller conveys a deed representing title to the property to a buyer for money or other consideration. The deed is then recorded in the county records establishing the new owner's right in the chain of title. The ceremony in which the title is conveyed is called the closing and hearkens to medieval times. In most real estate transactions the buyer cannot produce all of the sales price at closing. In such a scenario the seller could take back a mortgage entitling him to the property if the buyers fail to meet their commitment to pay.

Since sellers seldom want the burden of waiting years to be paid, most land transactions today involve financing by a bank or other lending institution. The lender in effect pays off the seller and assumes the seller's right to payment and to reenter the property upon default. Thus, at a minimum, most transactions involve a buyer, a seller, and a lender. A lawyer may represent any one of these parties in a transaction. Complex commercial real estate deals frequently involve a number of parties and a concomitant array of lawyers. Many real estate transactions also involve a real estate agent who brings together the buyer and the seller.

Traditionally, one of the lawyer's most important functions was to review the chain of title to certify that the seller actually held a good title to convey. A flaw in the title could mean at worst that the buyer received nothing, but in many cases meant that the buyer took the title subject to other restrictions. Today, most lawyers do not certify a title directly to buyer, but rather through a title insurance company that issues a title policy promising to pay the buyer if the title fails. In many states, title companies have taken over the bulk of residential real estate conveyances.

Commercial

Commercial transactions, because of their complexity, usually involve lawyers experienced in such matters. In simple residential transactions, however, lawyers have increasingly been cut out of the loop by title companies, which, although they are nonlegal corporations, are frequently owned, operated, and staffed by lawyers. Real estate transactions represent a multi-billion dollar industry, so the stakes for control of this lucrative market are high.

Commercial real estate often starts with a developer who conceptualizes a commercial project. The developer, like a movie producer, must bring together all the necessary players to make the deal work. Acquisition of the land is often a minor part of the process; if the developer already owns the land, it may not be an issue at all. The developer will need to retain engineers and architects to design the project. The developer will have to identify those who will be using the property as tenants, joint venturers, or owners after the project is completed. The developer will have to conduct environmental impact studies, satisfy the concerns of local residents, and secure local zoning and subdivision approval for the project. This process may take years. After the project has been approved, the developer must retain a general contractor to execute the design of the project. Frequently, when construction is complete, the developer gets out of the project and moves on to a new development. In many cases, however, the developer maintains an interest in the project either financially or through some management role. It would be almost impossible to complete even the simplest commercial real estate transaction without the assistance of lawyers. And because the stakes are so high, it is not uncommon for almost everyone involved in the process to be represented by legal counsel.

Zoning and Land Use

As mentioned above, zoning considerations can play an important role in commercial real estate transactions. They may be a factor in residential transactions as well. Zoning is but one part of a larger subspecialty of property law that can be described as *land use planning*. There was a time when owners of land could do almost anything they wanted with their land, subject to certain duties to those who came on the land and to those who were injured by instrumentalities that escaped from the land. Over the years the power of owners to use their land without restriction has diminished. Nineteenth century range wars between cattlemen and sheepherders over fencing the open range represent an early battle over land use. Since then, competing interests have clashed repeatedly over land use plans. As urbanization placed more people in proximity to one another, legal rights of property owners inevitably clashed. Recognition that space is limited and that many resources are scarce has placed additional burdens on owners. Today, questions of land use planning have significant impact and frequently extend far beyond an individual owner's decisions about use of a particular parcel of land. Government as well as private lawyers practice land use law at every level in every jurisdiction. For further information on this subject see Chapter 11 on environmental law.

WILLS AND TRUSTS

Another fundamental tenet of Anglo-American property law is the right of individuals to freely dispose of their property at death. The law in each state specifies the circumstances under which an individual can execute a will. Upon the death of the individual (the testator), the will can be admitted to probate, that is, submitted to the jurisdiction of a probate court. The court will appoint an executor or administrator to carry out the testator's final wishes with regard to the property. Although the executor is usually named in the will, the court retains the power to substitute executors under certain circumstances. If there is no will or if the will is invalid, the court may distribute the deceased person's property according to the state statute of descent and distribution.

Because both state and federal governments impose taxes on either the estate or the inheritance, a major focus of wills and estates practice involves minimizing the tax burdens. Since little can be done after the testator has died, it is important to take steps prior to death to accomplish this objective. The process of devising a testamentary scheme that maximizes the size of the inheritable estate actually distributed to the heirs is called *estate planning.* Lawyers who practice in this area must be familiar with both state and federal estate and income taxation.

A related area is the law of *trusts and trust administration.* Trusts are instruments that transfer the owner's use and enjoyment of property to a beneficiary while transferring legal title to a trustee charged with administering the property in the beneficiary's interest. At some point in the future, the trust transfers the entire interest in the property to an ultimate beneficiary. Trusts may operate either during the life or after the death of their creator. Whereas most trusts are drafted by lawyers in private practice, a large part of the trust administration business is handled by banks. It is not uncommon for lawyers to work in a bank trust department in the area of trust administration.

When the testator dies, the lawyer is often involved in taking the will through probate. This may involve admitting the will to probate, securing the appointment of an executor, settling disputes among the heirs, assisting in the distribution of assets, and closing the estate when all assets have been distributed. Probate matters can be so simple that they virtually require no lawyer assistance at all or so complex that they require years of litigation. Although there is no guarantee that for probate the heirs will bring the testator's will to the same lawyer who prepared it, most lawyers hope that this will happen, since the financial rewards of a state administration are usually much greater than those for will preparation.

HOUSING

Housing law has emerged as a significant area of practice, especially in areas where large numbers of people rent their homes. The English common law contained rules governing the rights and responsibilities of both landlords and tenants, but these laws were often tipped heavily in the favor of the landlords. They were also created for more simple agrarian times. Since the 1960s, tenants' rights advocates in many jurisdictions have been able to secure legislation protecting tenants' interests from abuses by landlords. Despite these laws, millions of people still live in substandard housing, and many tenants do not understand their rights. A significant number of housing cases involve low income, working class people or students. In some areas, many rental units have been converted to condominiums (where individuals own their unit) or cooperatives (where each person owns a share of the entire building). This affects the practice of law in two ways. First, it has given rise to an entire new body of law involving the rights of coop and condo owners and their boards of directors, management companies, and developers. Secondly, as apartment buildings are converted to individual ownership, the availability of affordable housing dries up. This problem is particularly acute in New York City and other older cities with a large number of apartment buildings. But it can also be a problem in fast-growing areas where the influx of new population outstrips the availability of housing.

LEASING

A final practice area that may be classified under property law is leasing. Although the term leasing can be used in the context of real property (e.g., Farmer Jones leased a field from Preacher Bob to grow corn), the most dramatic changes in leasing practices have involved personal property from cars to photocopiers to heavy industrial equipment to furniture. Businesses as well as individuals frequently elect to use property for a limited period of time, paying the owner for its use, rather than purchasing the property outright. The producers of some products find it advantageous to lease rather than sell those products. For instance, the back of the computer software package often discloses that the software is being leased, not sold, and carries certain obligations (e.g., not to copy the software and give it away). Leasing law represents a growing practice area that will continue to evolve in the coming decade.

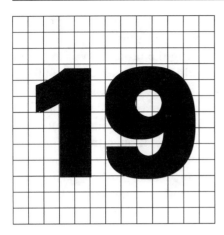

PUBLIC INTEREST

The field of public interest law encompasses a wide variety of different legal activities. In one sense, the term public interest is difficult to define, because different people have a different concept about what the public interest is. Conservatives want a free market and regulated speech; liberals want free speech and a regulated market. Everyone, it seems, has a personal view of what the public interest is.

Special interest groups with political agendas pursue their political interests in lieu of a broad party platform. These special interest groups may view their activities as furthering the larger public interest. Sometimes the interests involved clash dramatically, as in the case of abortion where pro-choice and pro-life forces struggle for the hearts and minds of the nation.

Today, it would be nearly impossible to frame an objective definition of public interest law. It makes more sense to define it subjectively—in terms of those who claim to be doing public interest work. This definition may trouble public interest lawyers of the 1960s who would disclaim any kinship with right-wing activists of the 1990s. In a diverse, pluralistic society, however, the broader definition makes more sense.

Another problem with the area of public interest law is that it really involves many other substantive fields of practice: torts, contracts, property, criminal law, and others. In reality, public interest law is often defined by the clients themselves, whether they are individuals, a class of persons, an interest group, or the public at large. In the latter case, an interesting question is: who represents the public?

This chapter attempts to delineate the primary fields of public interest law. These include constitutional law, civil rights law, poverty law, consumer protection law, and law involving the protection of other interest groups. As suggested above it would be impossible to list all the interests encompassed by the term public interest.

Lawyers who work in public interest law may work for a publicly funded organization such as legal aid, a nonprofit association such as a political action committee, a law reform association, a think tank, or a citizens group. Many lawyers who work in private practice take on public interest cases on a non-fee-paying, or *pro bono publico,* basis. Frequently, these lawyers are personally interested in the causes they represent; sometimes, however, they represent clients for no fee simply because they believe those clients deserve representation. The tradition of public service and the bar is a longstanding one that is often overlooked by critics of the legal profession.

CONSTITUTIONAL LAW

As the name suggests, constitutional law involves the interpretation of the Constitution (typically the U.S. Constitution, although there is a body of state constitutional law as well). Under our form of government the Constitution delineates the powers granted to the various branches of government, to the states, and reserved to the people. The Constitution sets forth a broad framework of rules, but leaves many questions of interpretation unanswered. Although the Constitution itself does not specify who should interpret its terms, Chief Justice John Marshall in *Marbury v. Madison* concluded that this was the ultimate responsibility of the judicial branch, settling the question for future generations. The body of constitutional law that has evolved during the nineteenth and twentieth centuries has provided a livelihood for countless lawyers.

Some of the multitudinal issues that fall within the framework of constitutional law are the power of the President to refuse to submit to a subpoena from Congress, a woman's right to have an abortion, the freedom under the first amendment to burn the American flag, the right of indigent criminal defendants to be represented by appointed counsel, the right of a lawyer to be licensed to practice law in a state where she does not reside, the obligation of states to compensate individuals for taking their property for public use, the power of states to impose the death penalty, and the right of public schools to require student prayer. A large number of cases define individual rights in relation to government power under the Constitution and Bill of Rights. Over the last one hundred years, the Supreme Court has frequently stricken down legislation that violates the Constitution. Jim Crow laws that tended to exclude southern blacks from exercising their voting rights are an excellent example of this type of law.

Constitutional law is exciting and challenging. It has the potential to affect significantly the way people live. It is constantly changing. Unfortunately, most lawyers see very few constitutional law cases after they get out of law school. The number of lawyers who practice constitutional law exclusively is limited, in part because there is very little money in constitutional law. Additionally, constitutional cases if they are appealed to the United States Supreme Court can take years. And the result can be disappointing. Thus, the lawyers who practice in this area are often motivated by a belief in the clients and causes they represent.

CIVIL RIGHTS

Civil rights law may be viewed as a subset of constitutional law, although many civil rights have been articulated as much through legislation as through judicial decision. Civil rights law involves representing individuals and groups whose rights have been infringed by others or by the government. Since the government may legitimately restrict a number of rights under the Constitution, determining the validity of such State action is an important element of civil rights practice. Cases involving racial discrimination have a long history in civil rights law. The infamous *Dred Scott* decision of 1857 that contributed to the outbreak of the Civil War was a civil rights case. In more recent years, women, handicapped persons, and gays and lesbians have also sought protection for their civil rights under the Constitution through legislation, court actions, or both.

POVERTY LAW

A large number of Americans lack the financial resources to support themselves with a decent standard of living. Without addressing the sociological roots of poverty, it is important to note that poor people have legal rights, too. They often lack the resources to retain legal counsel to vindicate these rights. Much of the poverty law in this country is practiced in publicly funded legal aid and public defender associations. Before 1970, many of these organizations were private charities that operated with the benefit of contributions from others. In the 1970s, Congress created a national Legal Services Corporation charged with consolidating these legal services programs into a national service. This objective has not been totally successful, as funding cuts have limited the scope of legal services activities.

Many poverty lawyers engage in the process of law reform, lobbying for favorable legislation, pursuing high impact litigation, and consciousness-raising community activities. The more political elements of law reform activities have drawn criticism when conducted by legal services attorneys. Funding for legal services to low income and indigent clients has been restricted in recent years, and law reform activities have fallen to citizens groups and watchdog agencies.

As is the case with constitutional law and civil rights, poverty lawyers tend to be rewarded personally rather than financially. Where poverty law programs can pursue fee-generating cases (e.g., court actions) they may be able to overcome public funding shortfalls. Individual lawyers, however, who are paid on salary scales at or below those of government lawyers usually do not benefit from such windfalls as their counterparts in private practice would.

CONSUMER PROTECTION

The broad field of consumer protection has developed out of the modern commerce associated with marketing products. Consumer protection has been spurred on by the growing awareness of the buyers and users of products concerning safety and usefulness. The consumer protection movement has also paralleled the development of product liability law holding manufacturers and distributors strictly liable for injuries caused by products placed in the stream of commerce. Consumer protection lawyers may be engaged in a number of different activities. They may be involved in product evaluation and testing either through informing the public about product defects or taking legal action to remove such products from store shelves; they may engage in lobbying activities aimed at producing legislation that guarantees consumer rights; they may sue companies over issues such as inaccurate labeling, misleading advertising, or inadequate product support. These legal challenges may also be pursued through the various government agencies charged with regulating the industries involved. Lawyers may also be involved in product liability litigation to seek recovery for individuals who have been injured through the use of defective products. Whether they work as individuals, members of law firms, directors or employees of public interest groups, legal aid organizations, or as representatives of government agencies, many lawyers encounter opportunities in this developing area of law.

REPRESENTATION OF OTHER INTEREST GROUPS

Lawyers find themselves involved in representing a large number of interest groups in society. Their activities, as with consumer protection lawyers, involve education, lobbying, and litigation. Just a few of the specialized public interest citizens groups that fall under this category are: historic preservation, animal rights, older citizens and retired persons, students, and the homeless. The existence of these fields of representation give evidence to the fact that the American legal system provides representation to every conceivable interest group. Many of these groups are not well funded and the individuals who comprise them are not wealthy. Although the scales of justice are not always evenly balanced, public interest lawyers have gone far towards equalizing the conditions.

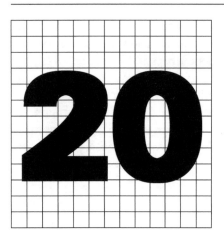

TAXATION

If there are only two inevitable things in life, death and taxes, then probably tax lawyers do not come far behind. Taxation is the process by which governments fund their operations through payments by individuals and businesses in society. Tax policy involves decisions about who, what, and how much to tax. In addition to raising money for governmental operations, the tax laws tend to affect social policy. For example, when federal income tax law was revised in 1987, deductions for interest on credit cards were phased out while deductions for interest on home mortgages were retained. The result is that people were discouraged from amassing large long-term debts on their credit cards in favor of taking second mortgages on the equity in their houses. Most people are more aware of taxes as they apply directly to themselves than to the effects of tax policy. Tax lawyers, in representing their clients, must be aware of both.

Tax law is a longstanding legal specialty. As the tax laws have become more complicated, the significance of tax practice has increased. Tax practice has a close relationship with public accountancy, and many tax lawyers are also CPAs. In fact, a substantial number of lawyers work in public accounting firms rather than law firms. Such lawyers, however, are prohibited from practicing law while in their capacity as employees or partners of accounting firms. Lawyers who practice tax law may be found in private law firms, corporations, associations, and, of course, the government. A traditional career path for many tax lawyers is to work for the Internal Revenue Service, the Justice Department Tax Division, or a state taxation agency before joining a law firm.

Other lawyers develop expertise in the field through postgraduate LLM tax programs. Some experience or education beyond a basic tax course in law school is inevitably necessary in order to be able to practice tax law. At the same time, separate licensure of tax lawyers has never been required.

This chapter attempts to dissect tax practice into categories the reader may not have considered previously. Although these categories may contain numerous subcategories, the areas covered represent the main branches of tax practice. These include: government practice, individual tax practice, corporate tax practice, pension and retirement tax practice, and estate tax practice.

GOVERNMENT TAX PRACTICE

Many tax lawyers at some point in their careers will work for one of the government agencies charged with administering the tax laws. Although the tax bureaucracy is large and lawyers may work in many positions within it, probably the most important role for lawyers in the process is in the area of enforcement. The tax audit procedure is designed to resolve informally disputes concerning the amount of tax owed between the taxpayer and the government. This process is similar whether it involves the IRS, a state department of taxation, or some other authority empowered to collect taxes. If the taxpayer and the agency cannot resolve the dispute over payment, the agency may elect to proceed to collect the tax deficiency.

The job of representing the agency in these cases falls to lawyers who represent the agency in formal hearings, suits to collect the judgment, and appeals. If it is determined that the taxpayer owes money, the lawyer may be involved in the collection process, placing liens on property, garnishing wages, and levying the judgment. In many of the cases involving disputes that are not resolved informally, the taxpayer will be represented by independent counsel. It is important, therefore, for the state to be represented by counsel as well. Another part of the enforcement process involves criminal prosecution for tax evasion, the willful nonpayment of taxes owed. At the federal level, criminal tax practice is handled through the Justice Department Tax Division. This is not always true at the state level. Since the gangster Al Capone was imprisoned for tax evasion in the 1930s, the tax laws have been used increasingly as a weapon in the fight against organized crime. Criminal tax practice has a special appeal for some lawyers because it implicates both tax and criminal law practice.

Lawyers who remain in the IRS or state tax department may find that in order to move up the career ladder, they must shift from purely legal work to administrative work outside the law. Many lawyers assume an adjudicative role by becoming hearing officers for the agency. In the federal government there is a special administrative Tax Court that hears tax appeals. Some practitioners may eventually secure appointment as judges in the Tax Court.

PERSONAL INCOME TAXATION

By far the largest area of tax involves personal income tax. Since every man, woman, and child who earns more than a negligible amount of money must file income taxes, there are millions of potential tax cases. There are millions of tax audits and hundreds of thousands of enforcement actions involving taxpayers. It should not be surprising that representation of these taxpayers would be a very large business. Many individuals utilize their lawyers in the planning stages in order to lower their tax obligations. Although lawyers share tax planning work with accountants, only lawyers can represent clients before the IRS, Tax Court, or other tribunal. Tax practice tends to involve individuals with substantial wealth or income.

BUSINESS TAX PRACTICE

In the business world, taxation is an important consideration in many corporate decisions. Since corporations and other businesses must pay taxes, many, just like wealthy individuals, use lawyers to help them reduce the size of their tax bills. There are special tax regulations for corporations, small (subchapter "S") corporations, partnerships, unincorporated associations, and nonprofit organizations. Because of these detailed regulations, business tax practice is a highly technical area requiring significant expertise.

PENSION AND RETIREMENT TAX PRACTICE

Although in some ways pension and retirement plans fall under the domain of business practice, they are also administered for the benefit of individuals. The Internal Revenue Code establishes complicated regulations for companies that offer pension and retirement plans for their employees. The drafting of such plans requires sophisticated legal work in order to meet the objectives of the company within the bounds of the law. For many individuals who are sole proprietors of businesses or whose employers do not offer retirement plans, it may be necessary to create individual retirement plans. One of the major questions throughout this area is when should deferred income be taxed? Because of the technical nature of this work, lawyers who handle pension, benefit, and retirement plans have developed their own subspecialties of the practice. Some of these, such as ERISA, are extremely narrow in their focus.

One subspecialty, sometimes not even considered to be a part of tax practice, is social security law. The nation's social security trust fund is funded through taxes paid by all workers, with benefits paid to qualified retirees. As in other segments of the tax field, the regulations are very complicated and require special understanding to interpret them. Lawyers who practice in the social security area often deal with retirees, disabled individuals, and other qualified individuals. The work may involve securing benefits for their clients, clarifying payments, or determining government obligations to pay in light of other retirement plans and income. For instance, social security regulations limit the amount of income that a retired person may earn from a job and still receive social security benefits. An elderly person working at a fast food restaurant must consider carefully the income caps in order to avoid losing benefits. The clientele in this social security area often involves lower income individuals, where social security is the major source of income. (See also Chapters 10 and 19 on elder law and public interest.)

ESTATE PLANNING

The state not only collects taxes on our income while we are alive, but also taxes the property we leave behind when we die. Estate planning is simply the process by which individuals make decisions about the disposition of their wealth prior to death in order to reduce the amount that goes to the government through estate taxes. At death, estate tax laws come into play, and the deceased can no longer change his obligations. The attorney for the estate, however, may be able to influence the amount of tax paid through favorable evaluation of property, distribution of assets outside the estate, and arguing to reduce the government's determination of the tax owed. As in other areas, professionals besides lawyers may be involved in the planning work, but only lawyers can represent others in probate court. Estate tax lawyers may represent heirs or creditors as well as the estate of the deceased.

An interesting subspecies of estate planning involves charitable contributions and deferred giving. One way to avoid paying estate taxes is to give away wealth before death. The tax laws allow a limited amount to be turned over to family members as gifts. They also provide for other situations when tax-free *inter vivos* (during the lifetime) gifts may be permitted. Qualified charitable and nonprofit organizations may be the subject of such gifts, and benefactors can give large amounts to such groups. Often, lawyers working for such charities have an expertise in charitable and deferred giving, so that they can help benefactors draft instruments to provide such gifts within the framework of the tax laws. Where the donor wishes to retain control of her wealth during life, it may be possible to draft will provisions making the charitable contribution at death in such a way as to avoid some of the taxes. A device used in many of these cases is a charitable trust created for the benefit of the designated beneficiary.

THE GENERAL PRACTITIONER AND THE SPECIALIST

Because taxation is so pervasive, it intrudes into the lives of all citizens in some way or another. It is hard to imagine any lawyer who will not encounter at least some tax problems during the course of a legal career. More likely they will face tax questions on a fairly regular basis. For this reason, all lawyers need to have a basic understanding of personal income, business, and estate taxation. They should know at least enough to be able to refer complicated tax questions to an expert when appropriate. To fail to do so may be malpractice. It may also be malpractice to attempt to handle highly complex tax matters without sufficient expertise. Thus, there is a broad-based need for tax specialists. This chapter suggests that the field of taxation can be divided into many very narrow subspecialties. Tax lawyers are a special breed, but for those who are interested in the field there are many varied opportunities for career choices.

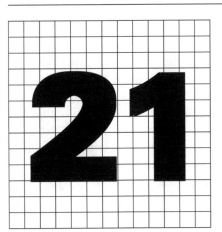

TORT LAW

The field of tort law is a broad one. In fact, torts represent not one cohesive theory, but a number of distinct legal actions. The word "tort" derives from the old French word for "wrong," and seems to have entered Anglo-American jurisprudence by way of the Normans. Over the years, tort remedies evolved as civil actions to compensate injured persons. Originally, there may have been a close link to the criminal law, at least as a means of punishing wrongdoers, but over the years tort remedies came to focus more on compensation than punishment.

Today tort cases proceed on one of three basic theories: (1) *intentional* torts, where the defendant intended conduct that injured the plaintiff; (2) *negligence,* where the defendant breached a duty to act with reasonable care and caused the plaintiff's injury; and (3) *strict liability,* where the defendant, for policy reasons, is held responsible for the plaintiff's injuries regardless of fault. Although there are many kinds of torts from personal injury to business torts, liability always rests on one of these theories.

This chapter describes some of the major forms of tort practice. Tort law is a widespread practice area because people can be injured anywhere. Tort lawyers may represent injured plaintiffs, defendants charged with liability, or insurance companies. Because many defendants are corporations such as manufacturers or distributors of products, or insurance companies protecting individuals against specified risks, defense practice is concentrated in larger law firms and in-house legal departments. Plaintiffs tend to be represented by individual practitioners or small firms specializing in tort law. Because personal injuries and other tort problems are so pervasive, almost every lawyer in private practice will encounter some work in this field. The practice is litigation-intensive, however, so many generalists prefer to refer tort cases to those specialized in trying them. The unique contingency fee structure in the tort area, where plaintiffs' lawyers take a percentage (typically one third) of the recovery if they win or settle, and nothing if they lose, can be very lucrative or unprofitable depending on the success of a lawyer's practice. Typically, tort lawyers represent either plaintiffs or defendants, but the separation of plaintiff and defense practice is not as rigid as it is in some areas of law such as labor.

NEGLIGENCE

The broad area of negligence law is usually referred to in practice as personal injury or PI. As the name suggests, personal injury law involves injuries to individuals brought about by someone else's carelessness. The law imposes a duty on everyone to act with reasonable care in carrying out activities that pose a risk of injuring other people. A breach of such duty causing injury and damages is the basis of negligence liability. Negligence cases can range from a slip and fall on a banana peel in the grocery store to airline crashes involving mass destruction. The largest number of PI cases involve automobile accidents or traffic. No single device has wrought as much widespread personal injury as the automobile. And yet this form of transportation is indispensable to modern life. Since automobile insurance is a factor in most accidents, insurance defense litigation makes up a significant part of PI litigation. Interestingly, most automobile accident cases, as well as other negligence cases where insurance is involved, are settled prior to trial. Thus, negotiation skills are as important as litigation skills for attorneys who practice in this area. A typical career path for many lawyers is to shift from prosecutorial criminal law practice to plaintiffs' personal injury practice. In addition to utilizing many of the same skills, these lawyers frequently view themselves as representing the same interests, those of the victim.

MALPRACTICE

A specialized but important offshoot of negligence practice is professional liability or malpractice. The idea behind professional liability is that those who have special training and expertise should exercise the degree of care in dealing with patients or clients commensurate with other members of the calling. For example, for the purposes of treating injuries a doctor is held to the standard of care of other doctors similarly situated rather than the standard of care of someone who has not been to medical school. It is no secret that malpractice litigation has mushroomed in recent decades. The willingness of injured people to sue professionals has provoked widespread controversy. Injured plaintiffs are no longer willing to sit back and endure careless mistakes of those in whom they entrust their lives and fortunes. Defendants and insurance companies claim that increased litigation drives up the cost of services and drives competent professionals out of the business. Although these questions cannot be answered in this book, the prospective lawyer may want to consider the social policy considerations inherent in this debate. Rhetoric sometimes casts the question in terms of pro- or anti-lawyer sentiment, but this is not an accurate characterization, because lawyers represent partisans on both sides of the issue. The real questions involve how and when injured persons should be compensated for injuries and when they should bear the risk of loss themselves.

The largest segment of malpractice litigation involves doctors. It is not the case that doctors must always be correct, only that they make reasonable judgments under the circumstances. Doctors are also required to inform patients of the potential risks of a particular proposed course of treatment. In medical malpractice, as well as other forms of professional liability, expert testimony is usually required to establish the elements of the plaintiff's case. In order to show what a reasonable doctor would have done, the plaintiff's lawyer must introduce testimony from another doctor to that effect. Because of this requirement and the complexity of medical problems themselves, malpractice litigation can be an extremely complicated business. As with other areas of tort law, insurance is almost always present, and settlement of claims occurs far more often than jury trials.

Although medical malpractice dominates the professional liability field, other professionals are increasingly subject to suits by their clients. Lawyers, accountants, ministers, teachers, and other professionals have successfully been sued for malpractice. Even in areas that have not traditionally been recognized as professions, individuals holding themselves out as possessing superior expertise have been held to the standards they profess. Thus, a plumber may hold himself out to the public as knowing more about how to fix pipes than ordinary laymen. He cannot be heard to complain that he did as good a job as an ordinary person when his plumbing job is done poorly, compared to the work of other plumbers. In this environment, everybody who possesses special knowledge or qualifications (and probably charges higher fees accordingly) should understand the professional standard to which they will be held under the law and should obtain insurance to protect against the risk of malpractice.

PRODUCT LIABILITY

The field that is now termed product liability law evolved over the years out of negligence. Historically, as the industrial revolution produced machines and other products that made both work and living easier, injuries related to these products increased. For much of the nineteenth century, the law was stacked heavily in favor of product manufacturers. This was due in part to the public policy favoring industrial and economic growth; but it was also related to the inability of legal principles established in medieval nonindustrial times to cope with the problems of the industrial revolution. Work-related injuries eventually were covered by workers' compensation laws that spread the losses due to injuries among employers—regardless of fault. The idea was that such costs could be borne more easily by employers who would profit by their industrial activity than by workers whose injuries often cut off any form of livelihood.

The problem was not as easy when it came to consumers injured by products sold on the open market. As for immediate purchasers of products from manufacturers, the producers of the product could contractually disclaim any warranties or promises concerning product safety. Product users who did not actually purchase the product were said not to be in *privity of contract* with the manufacturer, meaning that absent some contractual or other relationship, the manufacturer had no duty with respect to the user.

Even more problematic in many cases was the inability of injured parties to prove negligence in the manufacturing process. First, the manufacturer typically had exclusive access to the process of production. Second, the product frequently travelled through many hands—such as distributors and retailers—before reaching the user, and the conduct of any of these intervening parties could have been responsible for the injuries that resulted. Third, in many cases the conduct of the individual user was an issue because the doctrine of contributory negligence held that a plaintiff's own carelessness would bar recovery even if the defendant's conduct was negligent also. This meant that many injuries went without remedy. The courts, being generally sympathetic to injured plaintiffs, slowly developed theories to provide redress for these product injuries, first in the form of implied warranties that existed without regard to the contractual relationship between the parties, and then strict product liability.

The theory of strict product liability is fairly simple: One who places a defective product in the stream of commerce may be held liable to a purchaser or user of such product who is injured as a result of its use. As with work-related injuries, the public policy principle is that manufacturers and distributors who profit by the sale of products are in a better position to spread the risk of loss among all consumers as the cost of doing business than are individual product purchasers and users. While the basic concept of strict product liability is widely accepted today, there are wide variations in the law from jurisdiction to jurisdiction, and countless issues are subject to litigation as this field unfolds. For these reasons, product liability is one of the most active and dynamic areas of law practice in the country.

TOXIC TORTS

A variation of product liability, sometimes called toxic torts, incorporates strict product liability and environmental law. (See Chapter 11.) When a product is placed into the stream of commerce and proves to be toxic, it can produce extensive injuries. A drug taken by pregnant women may produce birth defects in their children or children's children; a defoliant sprayed on enemy sanctuaries during wartime may cause physical injuries to soldiers exposed to it; a common insulating material may later be found to produce cancer in those who live and work around it. These are just a few examples of the kinds of problems that may be classified as toxic torts. In the last example given, those injured are not product users but bystanders whose misfortune it is to be in the wrong place at the wrong time. Once again the law has been slow to recognize a remedy, but over time it has articulated a theory of liability to cover such injuries.

At the same time, in the environmental law field, courts were addressing similar problems involving bystanders injured by airborne pollution, toxic waste dumps, and contaminated waterways. Over time the scope of liability for injuries produced by toxic substances under nuisance and strict product liability theories has expanded. The question of how far liability should extend remains unresolved, as well as when the risk of loss should shift from the producer of the risk to the injured party.

DEFAMATION/PRIVACY/MISREPRESENTATION

Defamation

Another area of tort law that is actually ancient in origin is defamation. Whether written (libel) or oral (slander), defamation involves damage to a person's reputation. Although defamation came to America from the English common law, it has derived new vitality as an area of practice due to the interrelationship between traditional legal concepts and first amendment constitutional rights. Today, for example, a public figure must show not only that he was defamed but also that the defendant published the defamatory material "with reckless disregard for the truth." In short, freedom of the press and speech often conflict with an individual's right to control what is said about him.

Privacy

A related area of law, which has been recognized in recent years, is privacy. Here, the courts have recognized a group of interests, such as the right to be left alone and the right to exploit one's own image, that exist beyond the scope of the reputational interest. Privacy cases are often highly visible because they involve highly visible personalities.

Misrepresentation

A third group of "communication" torts involves misrepresentation and injurious falsehood. Whereas in most tort cases injury is caused by some physical action on the part of the defendant, in these cases the plaintiff is injured by words. In the case of injurious falsehood the words may not harm reputation or privacy interests but may do damage just the same. In misrepresentation the plaintiff has usually relied upon defendant's misrepresentation of material facts to the plaintiff's detriment. Many misrepresentation cases involve promises by sellers to buyers, and thus implicate contract law as well as torts. Although many of these cases are handled as contract problems under the Uniform Commercial Code, some injuries are more adequately redressed under tort theory.

BUSINESS TORTS

A growing area of tort law deals with business torts. Since corporations are entities, capable of suing and being sued, it follows that they can also injure and be injured. Not surprisingly, courts have had to deal with these issues. One of the more common types of business torts involves interference with contractual advantage. For example, two oil companies discuss a merger. After an agreement has been reached but before contracts are formally signed, a third company persuades the first to merge with it instead, to the detriment of the company left out of the deal. Look for suits like these to appear with increased frequency in the future.

INTENTIONAL TORTS

The last area of torts to be discussed in this chapter, although certainly not the last classification of torts, can be grouped together as intentional torts. These torts all involve intentional conduct by a defendant that injures a plaintiff. Intentional torts are the most ancient form of civil liability, emerging out of the criminal law long before negligence. They include trespass to land and chattels, conversion, assault, battery, and false imprisonment. In recent years, courts have also recognized the tort of intentional infliction of emotional distress. Although these actions make up a small portion of actual tort litigation, they are covered in depth in the first year torts class in law school, and they are not likely to disappear from the torts landscape in the future.

WHAT ELSE?

Although the descriptions included in this book are extensive, they are not exhaustive. A number of specialized practice areas have been discussed in other chapters as subcategories of major headings. Thus, ERISA practice referred to in the chapter on taxation (Chapter 20) is often referred to as a *boutique practice* area, but because it has been covered already, it will not be addressed in this chapter. The term boutique practice generally refers to a well-defined specialty practice area within the law. Often the term is used in the context of organizations providing specialized legal services, as in a boutique law firm. There are no hard and fast rules about when to classify a practice area as boutique. The boutiques described here do not fit neatly under any of the other chapter headings. A common thread running through all these descriptions is that they are readily identifiable as distinct segments of the lawyer population. Although many general practitioners may encounter problems in these areas, they lend themselves easily to specialty status because of their unique requirements. Boutique lawyers may practice alone, in a boutique firm, in a department of a larger firm, in a general practice, in a corporation, or in a government agency or other organization. There are obviously many boutique areas not described in this chapter, because they are so small or new. The areas described here, however, should give the reader a good sense of what constitutes a boutique practice.

AGRICULTURE

Much of the practice of law in small towns and rural areas involves representing clients who are farmers, ranchers, and others who make their living off the land. These individuals have unique legal problems, both in their personal affairs and their businesses. A simple estate planning problem encountered by many farmers is that a farm large enough to be economically viable may be extremely valuable. The income from the farm may be just enough to allow the farmer and his family to make ends meet. If the farmer dies, his estate, comprised primarily of land, may not be able to pay estate taxes without selling off the land.

Agricultural law also involves the legal problems of running an agribusiness, from acquiring farm equipment to producing a product and selling it for a profit on the market. While farming and ranching have traditionally been family businesses, an increasing number of corporations now compete with the family farmer. Farmers today deal with a host of government agencies from the EPA to the Department of Agriculture. These agencies have a say in everything from the use of fertilizers to crops planted to land set aside from planting.

While many agricultural lawyers are simply small town general practitioners, an increasing number of law practices devote substantially all their time to resolving the particular problems of those engaged in agricultural ventures. This is probably the single area of law practice that transpires predominantly outside of the major metropolitan centers.

AVIATION

Aviation law involves airplanes and air travel. Many aspects of aviation are governed by government regulations and agencies. Lawyers, whether representing the agencies, individual pilots and aircraft owners, airlines and their suppliers, or passengers may become involved with the regulatory process. Although regulation has diminished during the past decade, deregulation itself has raised legal issues and the need for legal representation.

Another aspect of aviation law is litigation involving injuries sustained in airplane crashes and other mishaps. Aviation cases constitute a highly specialized branch of personal injury litigation, often characterized by dealings with a common carrier (the airline), a defective product (the airplane), human error (the pilot or air traffic controller), and large numbers of human fatalities. Aviation lawyers frequently have experience as pilots or employees of an airline, although such a background is not specifically necessary.

SPORTS AND ENTERTAINMENT LAW

Sports and entertainment law has emerged as one of the more popular boutique practice areas in the country. Law students, perhaps hypnotized by the glamour and excitement of show business, were attracted in large numbers to the opportunities in sports and entertainment law. Unfortunately for these students, there was more hype than there were jobs. Just as with athletes and actors, out of the many who aspire to greatness only a few ever see their names in lights, and very few lawyers reach the top of the entertainment business.

Since sports, music, theater, and show business are different branches of the same industry, there are some common elements. Company lawyers represent teams, studios, and production companies. Other lawyers represent the players, actors, and musicians. Interestingly, many of these agents are not lawyers themselves, although many are. Nonlawyer agents periodically may be required to use separate legal counsel in work for their clients. Legal agents face unique ethical problems operating in an environment with nonlawyers who are not constrained by the same ethical duties.

In one sense, sports and entertainment law is basically contract law. All the parties to a transaction agree to perform certain functions in return for financial remuneration. The agreements governing these often complex productions are drafted and defended by lawyers. Not the least of the problems encountered by sports and entertainment lawyers is the difficulty of dealing with colossal egos who possess limited understanding of the law.

Lawyers in this field often engage in other areas of practice defined by their work setting. Thus, a lawyer for a motion picture studio may practice corporation law. An agent for a movie star may be involved in financial planning and investment for her client. Such investment may include independent production companies, restaurants, product endorsement, and a host of other ventures. Some of these lawyers also get involved in other areas of practice involving their clients, including criminal law, domestic relations, and defamation.

The overall picture to be drawn of sports and entertainment law presents a diverse field that is both exciting and challenging, but very small in numbers. Many of those who succeed in this business have contacts in the industry that predate law school, and those considering a career in entertainment law should begin at an early date to develop such ties.

ELECTION LAW

Election law is an area of practice that has developed with the increase in regulation of the electoral process in recent years. Federal, state, and even local election laws govern how candidates file and campaign for office, obtain contributions and other funding for their campaigns, and oversee the polling process. The election lawyer may spend as much time looking over the shoulders of the opposition as protecting the interests of his own candidate. Although heavy legal work tends to mount up in periods before elections, the election lawyer may be involved in some aspects of the process at all times.

Some lawyers represent political parties, political action committees (PACs), or oversight agencies. These lawyers frequently have administrative as well as legal responsibilities. Lawyers in the private sector may also be directly involved in the fundraising process as well. Periodically, election work will involve challenges to elections and other lawsuits growing out of the heated democratic process. Interestingly, many election lawyers become involved in this area of law because of their personal attraction to politics. As a result, for many, election law is a part-time pursuit or a vocation. The number of lawyers employed full time in the field of election law is limited, although since elections are national in scope, the practice exists in every corner of the land.

MARITIME/ADMIRALTY LAW

The law of the seas is sometimes called maritime law or admiralty law. For years, admiralty law and patent law were the only recognized areas of specialization in the legal profession. In the area of admiralty, this distinction arose because of a number of factors. First, legal problems on the water inevitably involved ships, and the sort of injuries that typically resulted (e.g., drowning) were clearly identifiable and often unique. Second, ships are usually involved in the commerce of moving cargo and passengers from one point to another. The transportation of such goods and people was subject to certain common risks (e.g., hurricanes). Third, maritime activities often implicated the interests and laws of different countries. Rivers as well as oceans may carry voyagers through the jurisdictions of several sovereign states as well as beyond the jurisdiction of any. Thus admiralty law, which is ancient in origin, has followed an independent course of development in the United States.

It should not be surprising that admiralty law has evolved its own rules and procedures, or its own specialized bar. Nor should it be surprising that admiralty law tends to be concentrated in cities by the water, particularly major ports. The area has grown in importance in recent years due to rising concerns about such environmental topics as offshore drilling, commercial fishing, and deep-sea dumping.

MILITARY LAW

The United States armed services represents millions of men and women in uniform plus their dependents, as well as a large number of civilian employees. Such institutions and large numbers of people could not exist without generating legal problems.

Both enlisted men and women and officers are covered by the Uniform Code of Military Justice, a document that defines the conduct of service people on active duty. To address traditional crimes as well as uniquely military forms of misconduct (e.g., disrespect to a superior officer), the Code provides not only for military courts but also for nonjudicial discipline imposed by a commanding officer.

Members of the armed services outside of the scope of their duties may be subject to civilian laws just as their dependents and military civilian employees are. At times, military and civilian jurisdictions overlap.

Lawyers for the military services may be involved in representing clients or prosecuting miscreants in the military judicial system, or representing service people or their dependents in actions involving the civilian law. Military lawyers also represent the military in actions such as contracts or where the military service itself is a party to litigation. Each armed service has a special branch known as the Judge Advocate General Corps that handles military legal work. Some of these lawyers eventually move on to become judges in the military court system, or commanding officers, but most military lawyers spend a four year tour of duty in the military before moving on to positions in civilian life.

DISCIPLINE

One final area of boutique practice that deserves mention is attorney discipline. All lawyers are governed by ethical rules. In most states they are in the form of Rules of Professional Conduct. Every state also maintains grievance committees comprised of volunteer lawyers to hear complaints that other lawyers have violated the Rules, and a paid professional staff of lawyers to prosecute disciplinary actions when appropriate. Although the number of lawyers who practice in this area is quite small, their influence over the lives of other attorneys is great. These disciplinary counsel are instrumental in defining and maintaining standards of professionalism and practice, and for this reason their importance cannot be minimized. Even though every law student must take a course in professional responsibility while in law school, very few actually consider a career in attorney discipline at the time. Taken together with bar association counsel, counsel to state bar examiners, and special counsel to other bar-related projects, the average attorney would be surprised at how many colleagues work for the legal profession itself.

In addition to voluntary work on disciplinary and other boards, many lawyers may find themselves involved in the disciplinary process representing lawyers against whom complaints have been filed. A related field is attorney malpractice, where lawyers may be involved not only in defending attorneys charged with malpractice but in representing clients who have been injured by an attorney's negligence. Although the two processes are sometimes confused by law people, the disciplinary process is designed to address violations of an attorney's responsibilities regardless of damages, while malpractice deals with negligence against a specific client resulting in injury.

FUTURE PROBLEMS

This chapter had sought to present descriptions of a variety of different specialty practices. It should be clear to the reader that these boutique areas are unique in that they involve special legal problems, identifiable clients, and unique services. It should also be clear that lawyers practicing in these areas require special knowledge, not only of the law, but also of the business or industry in which their clients work.

What may not be as clear from this reading is the slow movement in the legal profession away from general practice and towards specialization. Although lawyers may never become as rigidly specialized as doctors, it is safe to say that the number of lawyers who are true general practitioners is declining. Within law firms, lawyers are developing individual areas of expertise, and in large firms departmentalizing. In small firms, an increasing number of practitioners are turning away business outside their established areas of expertise. This trend shows no signs of retreating any time in the future. Prelaw students entering law school and the legal profession in the coming decade will undoubtedly become more than just lawyers, they will be lawyers whose identities are defined by substantive practice areas.

It may be even less clear to those who have not studied the legal profession to see that substantive specialties are always in a state of flux. New specialty areas are constantly emerging, and older specialty areas are dying out. This makes sense, considering the fact that lawyers' work involves solving people's problems, so if those problems change, the nature of the legal work will change as well. The lawyer of tomorrow thus will have to be a student of society as well as a student of law. The aspiring lawyer also may be able to make decisions in a somewhat different light when armed with this information about the nature of practicing law.

CONCLUSION

As the bulk of this book has made clear, there are countless careers in law. Individuals with legal training have a wide variety of career options available to them. When combined with extralegal skills and experience, law school graduates can work in many different roles.

At the same time there are many opportunities within the legal profession for individuals who do not have formal law school training. College students considering careers in law should not think that law school is their only option. There are advantages and disadvantages to going to law school. It may be possible to work in a law office or perform law-related work in many jobs where bar membership is not a prerequisite. Some states—such as California—are even tinkering with the idea of allowing certified paralegals to provide certain routine legal services directly to the public.

This book has described different facets of careers in law: the type of service rendered, the type of organization providing the service, the location of the organization and service, the substantive field of law, the critical skills required to perform the service, and the type of position or path. Look again at Chart 1 in the Introduction, which illustrates these facets graphically. Every career choice involves making a selection from one of the six facets. This book has demonstrated that there are numerous options under each. It follows that the number of permutations of these six facets and their options are extensive.

Obviously, not all options are equally easy to achieve. Not all of them offer the same rewards. Not all of them are good choices for any given individual. But there are so many options that it may be possible to find career satisfaction out there somewhere.

It is also worth noting that one is not limited to a single selection per lifetime. Many lawyers make major career moves by changing one or more of the six facets. Dissatisfied lawyers who leave the legal profession may change their careers one hundred eighty degrees. Others may make minor adjustments, changing locations or organizations. Evidence suggests that most lawyers will not stay in one place throughout their careers.

Ideally, career transitions should be logical. Each step should build upon past achievements. The skill facet is cumulative; one brings to each new position the sum of all the skills developed in past experiences. To toss out these skills can be disruptive as well as counterproductive to long-term success. A central objective of career planning should be to promote growth by building on the past. As simple as it sounds, this is not always easy to accomplish.

This book has dealt almost exclusively with career issues in terms of work. Work is not the only component to happiness. While job satisfaction contributes to happiness, it does not guarantee it. Additionally, personal considerations often play heavily in career choices and should not be ignored.

In his book *The Three Boxes of Life,* author and career counselor Richard Nelson Bolles talks about careers in the context of balancing three important components: learning, working, and playing. At different times during life, Bolles suggests, one of these "boxes" predominates, but at all times the well-rounded person must incorporate all three into his or her lifestyle.

This concept makes sense as an approach to legal careers as well. Justice Holmes once said "The law is a jealous mistress," meaning that it leaves little room for life outside of it. Commitment to the law, however, may produce a one-dimensional personality. It may also leave a lonely withered shell of a human being upon retirement. A career in law should be part of a full and rewarding life, not a prison or refuge from it.

As for learning, the process of continued growth is essential to long-term vitality. The old saying "you can't teach an old dog new tricks," is not consistent with Bolles' vision of life development.

A new generation of college graduates seems to recognize that balanced lives are most likely to result in satisfaction, not just in a career but in life. Lifestyle issues are important to many of them as they plan for families, recreation, jobs, and the demands of living.

Lawyers as a group have not always planned their lives to maximize happiness. The record of stress-related maladies, including divorce, alcoholism, drug abuse, and burnout, is not very good for lawyers. This does not have to be so. Although many forms of legal work can produce high anxiety, it does not follow that these career paths are necessarily debilitating.

The choice is an individual one. There are clear options for anyone going into the law. Finding a career path that brings satisfaction is important, but the larger goal of finding a lifestyle that produces happiness is more critical. For those about to embark upon a career in law, it will be necessary to spend some time thinking about these issues and then actualizing decisions.

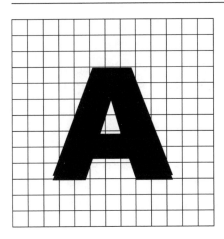

APPENDIX A: GLOSSARY

The following terms used in this book are defined in this glossary for easy reference by the reader. They not only define expressions used in the text, but also provide an easy guide to "legalese" with which many readers may not be familiar.

ABA—The American Bar Association. A national voluntary association of lawyers with a membership in excess of 300,000 members. The ABA is reputed to be the largest voluntary professional organization in the world.

ACCREDITED LAW SCHOOL—Although the term is sometimes used loosely, an accredited law school has been approved by the American Bar Association through an intensive inspection process; in most jurisdictions only graduates of ABA-approved schools may take the Bar Examination. Since the ABA is certified by the U.S. Department of Education to grant such approval, only ABA-sponsored schools can be considered accredited.

ADVERTISING—When used by lawyers, the term advertising generally refers to the right of lawyers to advertise to the public their availability to provide legal services as enunciated in the case of *Bates and O'Steen v. State Bar of Arizona.*

ALTERNATIVE PRACTICE—One of a number of areas of practice which are considered nontraditional. This definition is quite subjective, and the jobs included will vary depending on the individual. Usually alternative practice is a euphemism for legal aid, legal services, and public interest practice (and that is how it is used in this book), although some people also include any law-related employment not in a law firm.

ASSOCIATE—A junior lawyer in a law firm who is generally salaried, although some associates in some firms may participate in the earnings of the firm.

BACCALAUREATE DEGREE—The degree awarded at the completion of a four to five year college curriculum; a bachelor's degree (e.g., B.A., B.S., B.B.A., B.F.A., A.B.); the lowest educational level of degree held by students entering law school.

BAR EXAM—The test given to law school graduates before they are licensed to practice law; each state has its own bar exam, so law practice is limited to those jurisdictions in which an individual has passed the bar.

BILLABLE HOURS—The number of hours a lawyer works and charges to clients. Typically, lawyers keep time records of their work in order to establish a basis for their legal fees.

BY THE NUMBERS—In law school admissions, a practice by which applicants are considered solely on the basis of grade point average (GPA) and LSAT score, usually combined into an index. This method of selection may produce law school classes which have higher median scores with individuals in them who are less well-rounded, and arguably less qualified to practice law.

CAREER—The sum of an individual's working experience. Generally a career is thought of in terms of jobs, but should properly not be so limited.

CAREER DEVELOPMENT—The idea that a career has a direction or pattern that ideally should reflect the personal and professional growth of the individual over time.

CAREER OPTIONS—The choices available to persons in a professional field, generally those positions where one's education and experience prepare her or him for the work that will be involved on the job.

CAREER PLANNING—The concept of making rational career decisions on the basis of careful self-evaluation and analysis of the job market.

CLE—Continuing Legal Education. Programs offered to practicing lawyers to update or refine their skills in and knowledge of the law. Many states now require lawyers to meet mandatory continuing legal education (MCLE) requirements.

CLERKSHIP—1. A position held by a law graduate working for a judge for one to two years after graduation before taking a permanent job. 2. A summer or part-time job with a legal employer during law school doing research and other legal work for attorneys in the organization.

CLIENT—An individual who retains a lawyer, or a corporation, government, or other business organization utilizing a lawyer's services.

CLINICAL LEGAL EDUCATION—Courses in law school in which students handle actual legal problems under the supervision of professors or practicing lawyers instead of merely answering hypothetical or simulated problems; all law schools have some clinical programs but they vary widely in their size, scope, and orientation.

CONTRACTS—A branch of the law involving agreements among people and organizations, including when agreements are enforceable in law and what liability results from their breach; one of the primary first-year law school courses is contracts.

CORPORATE COUNSEL—A lawyer on the legal staff of a corporation.

ENTREPRENEUR—An individual who personally establishes and operates a business.

GENERAL COUNSEL—The chief lawyer in a business or government organization.

GPA—1. The college grade point average is used along with the Law School Admission Test (See LSAT) in selecting students to be admitted to law school. 2. The law school grade point average which legal employers often rely on when they hire new lawyers.

GROUP LEGAL SERVICES—Legal services provided to members of a group (e.g., an employees' union) by staff attorneys as a part of the benefits available to members of the group.

HANGING OUT A SHINGLE—Opening an individual office for the private practice of law.

HISHON—*Hishon v. King and Spalding.* A U.S. Supreme Court opinion holding that law firms may not discriminate against women in making available the opportunity to attain partnership in the firm.

HYPO—short for hypothetical situation, a case made up by the law professor to illustrate a point, deriving from hypothesis. Example—"Assume that I promise to give you $50 to walk across the Brooklyn Bridge and you agree. Now, when you get three fourths of the way across the bridge, I change my mind and revoke the offer. Can you sue me for the entire amount? For part of it? For your lost time?"

IN-HOUSE COUNSEL—In a corporation or agency or legal department, a lawyer who is on the staff of the corporation or agency, as opposed to outside counsel. A lawyer who works for a private law firm whose client is a corporation.

INTERNSHIP—A legal job during law school for which academic credit is given, and which usually involves supervision by a professor in addition to the practitioner employing the student.

JAGC—Judge Advocate General Corps. The legal arm of the military services.

J.D.—Juris Doctor—The basic law degree required to be completed in order to qualify to sit for the bar exam, usually requiring 3–4 years of study after graduation from college.

JOINT DEGREE—A program in which a law school offers a curriculum leading to degrees in law and another field, most commonly a graduate level degree in business administration.

JUDICIAL ADMINISTRATION—The management of the court system; a career involving such management.

LAW CLINICS—Law offices set up to provide inexpensive legal services to people of moderate means by routinizing and standardizing services in such a way as to lower costs while maintaining quality.

LAW FIRM—A group of two or more lawyers engaged in private practice of law; the owners of the firm are generally called partners or shareholders and the salaried lawyers, associates.

LAW-RELATED JOB—A job which is frequently filled by a lawyer and for which a legal education is valuable training, but which does not require that the law graduate holding the job be licensed to practice law by passing a bar exam.

LAW REVIEW—A journal published by a law school which contains academic analysis of legal questions and recent cases; the law reviews are student-edited by students selected on the basis of grades and/or writing competition.

LAWYERING SKILLS—Specific abilities that individuals who act as lawyers need to possess in order to provide legal services to clients.

LEGAL AID—A term frequently used to describe a program offering legal services to indigent or poverty level clients (See legal services).

LEGAL SERVICES—1. A general term used to describe the work that lawyers provide for clients (e.g., a lawyer is in the business of offering legal services to clients). 2. A more specific term used to describe a program offering legal services for indigent or poverty level individuals (e.g., the national Legal Services Corporation). Although used interchangeably with the term legal aid, legal services is becoming increasingly popular despite the confusing definition.

LITIGATION—An area of law practice involving the trial of lawsuits, the work also refers to any adversary trial in the courts where parties are represented by attorneys in an adversary relationship.

L.L.M.—Master of Laws—a postgraduate law degree obtained through 1–2 years of law school after the Juris Doctor (See J.D.).

LOCAL LAW SCHOOL—Euphemism describing a law school's reputation as neither a national nor regional school; a school where graduates usually obtain employment with legal employers from the metropolitan area where the school is located.

LSAT—The Law School Admission Test is an exam given to persons interested in attending law school. The LSAT is designed to test aptitude for doing legal work. While its effectiveness has been disputed, it is used as a major criterion for determining which applicants will be admitted to law school each year.

MEDIAN—The middle value in a set of ordered values; thus a median salary or LSAT score means that half the salaries or scores fall above and half below the median.

MODEL RULES OF PROFESSIONAL CONDUCT—A document promulgated by the American Bar Association nationally, and followed closely in the various states, which defines the lawyer's ethical responsibilities. Violation of these rules may lead to discipline by the authority which licenses attorneys, usually the Supreme Court of the state.

MOOT COURT—A law school activity involving a competition in which students write briefs and orally argue hypothetical cases before moot court judges.

NATIONAL LAW SCHOOL—Euphemism describing a law school's reputation as one of the elite law schools in the nation; a school whose graduates are recruited by legal employers from throughout the country.

NIGHT SCHOOL—Some law schools have a part-time program in the evening for students who must work their way through school; such a program normally takes four years to complete instead of three necessary for full-time students.

NO-FAULT—A system of compensation for victims of accidents which does not rely upon negligence as a basis of liability, and in so doing eliminates expensive personal injury litigation.

NONLEGAL JOB—A job in which a law graduate does not practice law or specifically use his/her law training. Law school may provide a general background and training for the position.

PARTNER—One of the members of a law firm; the partners are the owners of the business; the shareholders in a professional corporation are sometimes called partners.

PERSONAL INJURY—An area of law practice involving litigation produced as a result of some injury to an individual. PI, as it is called, usually involves negligence on the part of one of the parties, resulting in the injury to the other, and in most cases today insurance is involved.

POPULATION/ATTORNEY RATIO—The population of a given area divided by the number of attorneys in that area; a figure that is frequently used to assess the relative abundance of lawyers.

PRE-LAW MAJOR—A student in college who is preparing to attend law school. There are very few schools that offer a course of study in "pre-law" which would lead to a degree as in English or Business, so the term properly describes only the students themselves who may be in any field of study.

PREPAID LEGAL SERVICES—Legal services provided to persons or families who participate in a plan under which they make monthly contributions and receive benefits designed under the plan. Prepaid legal insurance works very much like Blue Cross/Blue Shield in the health field.

PRIVATE PRACTICE—An individual or organization engaged in the business of delivering legal services for compensation.

PRO BONO PUBLICO—(Latin—*for the public good*). A term sometimes used interchangeably with public interest, but also used to refer to the lawyer's responsibility to perform work in the public interest. The organized bar is divided as to the extent and limits of this responsibility.

PROPERTY—A branch of the law dealing with ownership of land, objects (chattels), ideas, or anything including what can be owned and what rights are associated with ownership; one of the primary first-year law school courses is property.

PROSECUTOR—A lawyer who works for a government office charged with prosecuting criminal cases on behalf of the state, including district attorneys, county attorneys, U.S. attorneys, and many city attorneys.

PUBLIC DEFENDER—The attorney who works in an organization engaged in the criminal defense of indigent clients. Since the U.S. Supreme Court case of *Gideon v. Wainwright* every person who is accused of a crime is guaranteed the right to legal representation. Many jurisdictions fund public defender offices for accused persons who cannot afford to retain private counsel.

PUBLIC INTEREST PRACTICE—A law practice in which the lawyer's clients are not normal paying individuals or corporations, but the public at large; in some cases certain special interest groups promote their causes as public interest (See also Pro Bono Publico).

REGIONAL LAW SCHOOL—Euphemism describing a law school's reputation as being recognized as having a regional reputation; a school whose graduates are recruited predominantly by legal employers from the region where the school is located.

SKILLS—In the career choice process skills are the things that you can do: think of them as action verbs and as transferable; they represent the things you will be required to do when working in a particular profession such as law.

SOCRATIC METHOD—A teaching method used in American law schools since the nineteenth century in which the professor, using either written decisions of appellate courts or hypothetical situations, teaches by means of intense questioning of students concerning the cases. Named for the Greek philosopher Socrates, who taught by using a question–answer format, and introduced into legal education at Harvard Law School in the 1870s, the Socratic method in recent years has been supplemented in most law schools by traditional lectures, practical or clinical programs, seminars, and problem-solving research courses.

SOLE PRACTITIONER—(also solo practitioner). An individual lawyer in a private practice.

SPECIALIZATION—The development of a practice of law limited to a narrow field of expertise, an increasing phenomenon in the legal profession today.

SUBSTANTIVE LAW—An area of law practice defined by its subject matter (e.g., energy law, admiralty law).

TAX LAW—An area of law practice which involves the complex and pervasive federal and state taxation laws.

TORT—(French N.—*Wrong*) An area of law dealing with injuries. While most tort law deals with negligent acts that result in injuries, there are also intentional torts and torts in which negligence need not be shown before liability can be established. One of the primary first-year law school courses is in torts.

UNDEREMPLOYED—A term referring to a person who believes that her or his job is not utilizing legal skills adequately. While this term clearly covers those who have accepted nonlegal jobs although they wanted legal ones, it can also be used to refer to anyone who is not satisfied with his or her present job.

UNEMPLOYED—In the legal profession, a person who is actively seeking a legal or law-related job but cannot find one and is not employed.

WORK VALUES—Those basic needs and attitudes that determine satisfaction in a professional career choice or job; for example, independence, power, wealth, altruism.

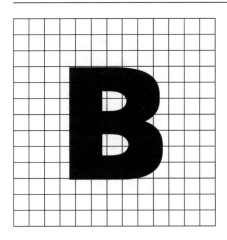

APPENDIX B:
NATIONAL ASSOCIATION
FOR LAW PLACEMENT
1995 EMPLOYMENT REPORT
AND SALARY SURVEY
PRESS RELEASE

FOR INFORMATION CONTACT:

Pam Malone, 1996–1997 President
Vanderbilt University School of Law
(615) 322-6192

Paula Patton
Executive Director
(202) 667-1666

Judith Collins
Director of Research and Information Resources
(202) 667-1666

EMPLOYMENT PATTERNS AND SALARIES FOR NEW LAWYERS SHOW MODEST GAINS

The National Association for Law Placement (NALP) has announced publication of the *Class of 1995 Employment Report and Salary Survey,* the only comprehensive reference document available on the employment experiences of recent law graduates. This 22nd consecutive report reveals the first increase in the full-time legal employment rate of new J.D. graduates since 1988, and only the second increase in the overall employment rate since 1987. Of the employed graduates reporting on their job status, nearly 82% indicated satisfaction with their job choice by responding that they were not currently seeking other employment.

A total of 165 ABA-accredited law schools responded to the survey, providing employment information on 83% of the graduates of the Class of 1995.

- Of those graduates whose employment status was known, 86.7% were employed six months after graduation, an increase of two percentage points over the Class of 1994, and only the second measurable increase since 1987. Despite the increase, however, that employment rate contrasts notably with rates as high as 92% in the late 1980s.

- Of those graduates whose employment status was known, just over three-quarters (76.1%) accepted legal positions, and 10.6% accepted non-legal positions. These rates compare favorably with the Class of 1994, when 74.8% of graduates for whom employment status was known were employed in legal positions and 9.9% were in non-legal positions.

- Employment in full-time legal positions was 70.7%, compared with 69.6% for the Class of 1994, the first increase since 1988. At the same time, relatively more graduates obtained full-time non-legal positions (9% versus 8.1%). These two increases contributed almost equally to and together accounted for the higher overall employment rate. Rates of part-time employment changed relatively little.

- As in all prior years that NALP has collected data, the most common employment setting was that of private practice within a law firm. Of graduates from the Class of 1995 who were known to be employed, 56.1% obtained their first job in a law firm, up from 55% for the Class of 1994. This is the first increase since 1988, when employment in law firms crested at 64.3%.

- Employment in business and industry was recorded at the highest level in the 22 years that NALP has been collecting data. The percentage of jobs taken in the business realm (13.4% for the Class of 1995) has more than doubled since 1989. In contrast, public service employment, including government jobs, judicial clerkships, and public interest positions, accounting for 26.6% of jobs taken by employed graduates, down from 27.9% in 1994.

- The median salary paid to members of the Class of 1995 for full-time jobs was $40,000, an increase of $3,000 over 1994. Private sector median salaries are higher than this overall median, at $50,000 in private practice and $43,000 in business and industry. The median for public service positions ranged from $30,000 for public interest jobs to $34,000 for judicial clerkships.

- The higher median in private practice notwithstanding, high salaries in this sector were the exception rather than the rule. Fewer than one in six law firm salaries was more than $70,000 and about 36% were $40,000 or less.

In addition to documenting the experience for the class as a whole, the report clearly demonstrates that employment experiences differ for graduates according to race, ethnicity, age, and gender.

- About 44% of employed African-American graduates accepted jobs in private practice, compared with 57% of employed white graduates and 54% of employed Asian/Pacific and Hispanic graduates. Conversely, government jobs accounted for over one-fifth of jobs taken by African-Americans, a rate nearly twice that of white graduates.

- Older graduates were less likely to go into private practice and more likely to enter academic or business settings. About 46% of employed graduates age 46 or older entered private practice, compared with 59.8% of employed graduates age 20–25. About one-fifth of employed graduates age 36 or older took jobs in business or industry, a rate well over twice that of employed graduates age 20–25.

- Almost one-third of employed women took government, judicial clerkship and public interest positions, compared with only one-quarter of employed men.

This year's *Employment Report and Salary Survey* includes new data that chronicle sources of jobs, timing of job offers, and the job satisfaction of employed graduates. This added feature offers valuable information for everyone interested in understanding the legal employment market for new graduates.

- By far the most frequently reported job source was a letter or other "self-initiated contact" with the employer. This source was reported for 29% of jobs. Although most jobs obtained through fall on-campus interviewing were law firm jobs, such positions were equally as likely to be obtained through a self-initiated contact.

- Just under two-thirds of jobs for which timing of offer was reported were received before graduation. The remainder were split relatively evenly between those obtained after graduation but before bar results and those obtained after bar results. These figures varied considerably among employer types, however. Law firm and judicial clerkship positions were most likely to be obtained before graduation. Among government positions, in contrast, only those with the military were typically obtained before graduation. Over half of the jobs in very small firms of 2–10 were obtained after graduation, and over one-quarter were obtained after bar results.

- Of the employed graduates for whom search status was reported, only 18.5% reported that they continued to seek another position. Among graduates seeking a different job, 42.8% were employed in full-time legal jobs. These figures varied depending on job and employer type, law school region, demographic factors, and job source, but reflect a generally high job satisfaction level among recent graduates.

The complete *Class of 1995 Employment Report and Salary Survey* provides more detail on these topics as well as additional topics, including salary levels and the nature of jobs by law firm size, level of government, and type of business; salaries for all states; all full-time legal salaries for 180 cities; geographic mobility of graduates; and employment patterns for selected cities and states. The report is available for $65 and may be obtained by contacting NALP at 1666 Connecticut Avenue, Suite 325, Washington, D.C. 20009, (202) 667-1666.

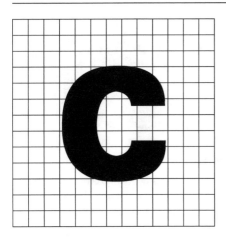

APPENDIX C:
SELECTED STANDARDS:
AMERICAN BAR
ASSOCIATION STANDARDS
FOR APPROVAL OF LAW
SCHOOLS AND
INTERPRETATIONS

Standard 208. NON-UNIVERSITY AFFILIATED LAW SCHOOLS.

If a law school is not part of a university or, although a part, is physically remote from the rest of the university, the law school should seek to provide its students and faculty with the benefits that usually result from a university connection, such as by enlarging its library collection to include materials generally found only in a university library and by developing working relationships with other educational institutions in the community.

Standard 209. LAW SCHOOL-UNIVERSITY RELATIONSHIP.

(a) If a law school is part of a university, that relationship shall serve to enhance the law school's program.

(b) If a university's general policies do not adequately facilitate the recruitment and retention of competent law faculty, appropriate separate policies should be established for the law school.

(c) The resources generated by a law school that is part of a university should be made available to the law school to maintain and enhance its program of legal education.

(d) A law school shall be given the opportunity to present its recommendations on budgetary matters to the university administration before the budget for the law school is submitted to the governing board for adoption.

Standard 210. EQUALITY OF OPPORTUNITY.

(a) A law school shall foster and maintain equality of opportunity in legal education, including employment of faculty and staff, without discrimination or segregation on ground of race, color, religion, national origin, sex, or sexual orientation.

(b) A law school may not use admission policies or take other action to preclude admission of applicants or retention of students on the basis of race, color, religion, national origin, sex, or sexual orientation.

(c) The denial by a law school of admission to a qualified applicant is treated as made upon the ground of race, color, religion, national origin, sex, or sexual orientation if the ground of denial relied upon is

(1) a state constitutional provision or statute that purports to forbid the admission of applicants to a school on the ground of race, color, religion, national origin, sex, or sexual orientation; or

(2) an admissions qualification of the school which is intended to prevent the admission of applicants on the ground of race, color, religion, national origin, sex, or sexual orientation though not purporting to do so.

(d) The denial by a law school of employment to a qualified individual is treated as made upon the ground of race, color, religion, national origin, sex, or sexual orientation if the ground of denial relied upon is an employment policy of the school which is intended to prevent the employment of individuals on the ground of race, color, religion, national origin, sex, or sexual orientation though not purporting to do so.

(e) This Standard does not prevent a law school from having a religious affiliation or purpose and adopting and applying policies of admission of students and employment of faculty and staff which directly relate to this affiliation or purpose so long as (i) notice of these policies has been given to applicants, students, faculty, and staff before their affiliation with the law school, and (ii) the religious affiliation, purpose, or policies do not contravene any other Standard, including Standard 405(b) concerning academic freedom. These policies may provide a preference for persons adhering to the religious affiliation or purpose of the law school, but shall not be applied to use admission policies or take other action to preclude admission of applicants or retention of students on the basis of race, color, religion, national origin, sex, or sexual orientation. This Standard permits religious policies as to admission, retention, and employment only to the extent that they are protected by the United States Constitution. It is administered as if the First Amendment of the United States Constitution governs its application.

(f) Equality of opportunity in legal education includes equal opportunity to obtain employment. A law school should communicate to every employer to whom it furnishes assistance and facilities for interviewing and other placement functions the school's firm expectation that the employer will observe the principle of equal opportunity and will avoid objectionable practices such as

(1) refusing to hire or promote members of groups protected by this policy because of the prejudices of clients or of professional or official associates;

(2) applying standards in the hiring and promoting of these individuals that are higher than those applied otherwise;

(3) maintaining a starting or promotional salary scale as to these individuals that is lower than is applied otherwise; and

(4) disregarding personal capabilities by assigning, in a predetermined or mechanical manner, these individuals to certain kinds of work or departments.

Standard 212. INDIVIDUALS WITH DISABILITIES.

A law school may not discriminate against individuals with disabilities in its program of legal education. A law school shall provide full opportunities for the study of law and entry into the profession by qualified disabled individuals. A law school may not discriminate on the basis of disability in the hiring, promotion, and retention of otherwise qualified faculty and staff.

Standard 213. CAREER SERVICES.

A law school should provide adequate staff, space, and resources, in view of the size and program of the school, to maintain an active career counseling service to assist its students and graduates to make sound career choices and obtain employment.

Chapter 3
PROGRAM OF LEGAL EDUCATION

Standard 301. OBJECTIVES.

(a) A law school shall maintain an educational program that is designed to qualify its graduates for admission to the bar and to prepare them to participate effectively in the legal profession.

(b) The educational program of a law school shall be designed to prepare the students to deal with both current and anticipated legal problems.

(c) A law school may offer an educational program designed to emphasize certain aspects of the law or the legal profession.

Standard 302. CURRICULUM.

(a) A law school shall offer to all students:

(1) instruction in those subjects generally regarded as the core of the law school curriculum;

(2) an educational program designed to provide its graduates with basic competence in legal analysis and reasoning, legal research, problem solving, and oral and written communication;

(3) at least one rigorous writing experience; and

(4) adequate opportunities for instruction in professional skills.

(b) A law school shall require of all students in the J.D. degree program instruction in the history, goals, structure, duties, values, and responsibilities of the legal profession and its members, including instruction in the Model Rules of Professional Conduct of the American Bar Association. A law school should involve members of the bench and bar in this instruction.

(c) The educational program of a law school shall provide students with adequate opportunities for study in seminars or by directed research and in small classes.

(d) A law school shall offer live-client or other real-life practice experiences. This might be accomplished through clinics or externships. A law school need not offer this experience to all students.

(e) A law school should encourage its students to participate in pro bono activities and provide opportunities for them to do so.

(f) A law school may offer a bar examination preparation course, but may not grant credit for the course or require it as a condition for graduation.

Interpretation 302-1:
Instruction in professional skills need not be limited to any specific skill or list of skills. Each law school is encouraged to be creative in developing programs of instruction in professional skills related to the various responsibilities which lawyers are called upon to meet, using the strengths and resources available to the school. Trial and appellate advocacy, alternative methods of dispute resolution, counseling,

*interviewing, negotiating, problem solving, factual investigation, orga-
nization and management of legal work, and drafting are among the
areas of instruction in professional skills that fulfill Standard 302(a)(iv).
(August 1996)*

Interpretation 302-2:

*A law school need not accommodate every student requesting en-
rollment in a particular professional skills course. (August 1996)*

Standard 303. SCHOLASTIC ACHIEVEMENT; EVALUATION.

(a) A law school shall have and adhere to sound standards of scholastic achievement, including clearly defined standards for good
standing, advancement, and graduation.

(b) The scholastic achievements of students shall be evaluated from
the beginning of the students' studies.

(c) A law school shall not continue the enrollment of a student whose
inability to do satisfactory work is sufficiently manifest so that the
student's continuation in school would inculcate false hopes, constitute economic exploitation, or detrimentally affect the education of
other students.

Standard 304. COURSE CREDIT; RESIDENT STUDY.

(a) A law school shall require, as a condition for graduation, successful
completion of a course of study in residence of not fewer than 1,120
class hours, including external study meeting the requirements of Standard 305, extending over not fewer than three academic years for a full-
time student or four academic years for a part-time student.

(b) An academic year shall consist of not fewer than 140 days on which
classes are regularly scheduled in the law school, extending into not
fewer than eight calendar months. Time for reading periods, examinations, or other activities may not be counted for this purpose.

(c) A law school shall not award full-time residence credit to a student who does not devote substantially all of the student's working
hours to the study of law or engages in employment for more than
20 hours per week, whether outside or inside the law school. Regular and punctual class attendance is necessary to satisfy residence
credit and class hour requirements.

(d) To receive full residence credit for an academic period, a full-
time student shall be enrolled for not fewer than ten class hours a
week and must receive credit for not fewer than nine class hours,

and a part-time student shall be enrolled for not fewer than eight class hours a week and must receive credit for all eight class hours. If a student is not enrolled in or fails to receive credit for the specified number of hours, the student may receive residence study credit only in the ratio that the hours enrolled in or in which credit was received, as the case may be, bear to the minimum specified.

(e) Pro rata credit for residence study may be awarded for study during a summer session on a basis that fairly apportions a student's effort to the usual residence period.

(f) A law school shall confer the J.D. degree contemporaneous with the time the academic requirements for the degree are completed.

(g) A law school shall not grant credit for study by correspondence.

Chapter 5
ADMISSIONS

Standard 501. ADMISSIONS.

(a) A law school's admission policies shall be consistent with the objectives of its educational program and the resources available for implementing those objectives.

(b) A law school shall not admit applicants who do not appear capable of satisfactorily completing its educational program and being admitted to the bar.

Standard 502. EDUCATIONAL REQUIREMENTS.

(a) A law school shall require for admission to its J.D. degree program a bachelor's degree, or successful completion of three-fourths of the work acceptable for a bachelor's degree, from an institution that is accredited by a regional accrediting agency recognized by the Department of Education.

(b) In an extraordinary case, a law school may admit to its J.D. degree program an applicant who does not possess the educational requirements of subsection (a) if the applicant's experience, ability, and other characteristics clearly show an aptitude for the study of law. The admitting officer shall sign and place in the admittee's file a statement of the considerations that led to the decision to admit the applicant.

Interpretation 502-1:
Before an admitted student registers, or within a reasonable time thereafter, a law school shall have on file the student's official transcript

showing receipt of a bachelor's degree, if any, and all academic work undertaken. "Official transcript" means a transcript certified by the issuing school to the admitting school or delivered to the admitting school in a sealed envelope with seal intact. A copy supplied by the Law School Data Assembly Service is not an official transcript, even though it is adequate for preliminary determination of admission. (August 1996)

Standard 503. ADMISSION TEST.

A law school shall require all applicants to take an acceptable test for the purpose of assessing the applicants' capability of satisfactorily completing its education program. A law school that is not using the Law School Admission Test sponsored by the Law School Admission Council shall establish that it is using an acceptable test.

Standard 504. CHARACTER AND FITNESS.

A law school shall advise each applicant to secure information regarding the character and other qualifications for admission to the bar in the state in which the applicant intends to practice. The law school may, to the extent it deems appropriate, adopt such tests, questionnaires, or required references as the proper admission authorities may find useful and relevant, in determining the character and fitness of the applicants to the law school. If a law school considers an applicant's character qualifications, it shall exercise care that the consideration is not used as a reason to deny admission to a qualified applicant because of political, social, or economic views which might be considered unorthodox.

Standard 505. PREVIOUSLY DISQUALIFIED APPLICANT.

A law school may admit or readmit a student who has been previously disqualified for academic reasons upon an affirmative showing that the student possesses the requisite ability and that the prior disqualification does not indicate a lack of capacity to complete the course of study at the admitting school. In the case of admission to a law school other than the disqualifying school, this showing shall be made either by a letter from the disqualifying school, or if two or more years have elapsed since that disqualification, by the nature of interim work, activity, or studies indicating a stronger potential for law study. In each case, the admitting officer shall sign and place in the admittee's file a statement of the considerations that led to the decision to admit or readmit the applicant.

Standard 506. APPLICANTS FROM STATE-ACCREDITED LAW SCHOOLS.

(a) A law school may admit a student with advanced standing and allow credit for studies at a state-accredited law school if:

(1) the studies were "in residence" as provided in Standard 304, or qualify for credit under Standard 305; and

(2) the content of the studies was such that credit therefor would have been granted towards satisfaction of degree requirements at the admitting school.

(b) Advanced standing and credit hours granted for study at a state-accredited law school may not exceed one-third of the total required by an admitting school for its J.D. degree.

Standard 507. APPLICANTS FROM FOREIGN LAW SCHOOLS.

(a) A law school may admit a student with advanced standing and allow credit for studies at a law school outside the United States if:

(1) the studies were "in residence" as provided in Standard 304, or qualify for credit under Standard 305;

(2) the content of the studies was such that credit therefor would have been granted towards satisfaction of degree requirements at the admitting school; and

(3) the admitting school is satisfied that the quality of the educational program at the foreign law school was at least equal to that required by an approved school.

(b) Advanced standing and credit hours granted for foreign study may not exceed one-third of the total required by an admitting school for its J.D. degree.

Standard 508. ENROLLMENT OF NON-DEGREE CANDIDATES.

Without requiring compliance with its admission standards and procedures, a law school may enroll an individual in a particular course or limited number of courses, as an auditor, non-degree candidate, or candidate for a degree other than a law degree

(1) a student enrolled in other colleges or universities or in other departments of the university of which the law school is a part; and

(2) a member of the bar, a graduate of other approved law schools, and other persons satisfying the requirements for admission set forth in Standard 502.

Standard 509. BASIC CONSUMER INFORMATION.

A law school shall publish basic consumer information. The information shall be published in a fair and accurate manner reflective of actual practice.

Interpretation 509-1:
The following categories of consumer information are considered basic:

(1) admission data;

(2) tuition, fees, living costs, financial aid, and refunds;

(3) enrollment data and graduation rates;

(4) composition and number of faculty and administrators;

(5) curricular offerings;

(6) library resources;

(7) physical facilities; and

(8) placement rates and bar passage data. (August 1996)

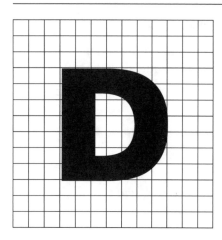

APPENDIX D:
U.S. LAW SCHOOLS APPROVED BY THE AMERICAN BAR ASSOCIATION

Source: *Law Services Information Book 1991–1992;* duplicates *AALS Directory*

University of Akron
School of Law
Corner Wolf Ledges and
    University Avenue
Akron, OH 44325-2901
216-972-7331

University of Alabama
School of Law
P.O. Box 870382
Tuscaloosa, AL 35487
205-348-5440

Albany Law School of Union
    University
80 New Scotland Avenue
Albany, NY 12208
518-445-2326

American University
Washington College of Law
4801 Massachusetts Avenue,
    N.W.
Washington, DC 20016
202-274-4101

University of Arizona
College of Law
Tucson, AZ 85721
602-621-3477

Arizona State University
College of Law
Armstrong Hall
Box 877906
Tempe, AZ 85287-0604
602-965-1474

University of Arkansas—
    Fayetteville
School of Law
Fayetteville, AR 72701
501-575-3102

University of Arkansas—Little
    Rock
School of Law
1201 McAlmont Street
Little Rock, AR 72202
501-324-9439

University of Baltimore
School of Law
1420 North Charles Street
Baltimore, MD 21201
410-837-4459

Baylor University
School of Law
P.O. Box 97288
Waco, TX 76798
817-755-1911

Boston College
Law School
885 Centre Street
Newton, MA 02159
617-552-9350

Boston University
School of Law
765 Commonwealth Avenue
Boston, MA 02215
617-353-3100

Brigham Young University
J. Reuben Clark Law School
342 JRCB
Provo, UT 84602
801-378-4277

Brooklyn Law School
250 Joralemon Street
Brooklyn, NY 11201
718-780-7906

University of California—
    Berkeley
School of Law
220 Boalt Hall
Berkeley, CA 94720
510-642-2273

University of California—Davis
School of Law
Kings Hall
Davis, CA 95616
916-752-6477

University of California
Hastings College of Law
200 McAllister Street
San Francisco, CA 94102
415-565-4623

University of California—Los
    Angeles
School of Law
71 Dodd Hall A 951445
Los Angeles, CA 90024
213-825-4041

California Western
School of Law
225 Cedar Street
San Diego, CA 92101
619-525-1401

Campbell University
Norman Adrian Wiggins School
    of Law
Box 158
Buies Creek, NC 27506
918-893-1200

Capital University
Law School
665 South High Street
Columbus, OH 43215
614-445-8836

Benjamin N. Cardozo
School of Law
Yeshiva University
55 Fifth Avenue
New York, NY 10003
212-790-0274

Case Western Reserve University
School of Law
11075 East Boulevard
Cleveland, OH 44106
216-368-3600

Catholic University of America
School of Law
Cardinal Station
Washington, DC 20064
202-319-5151

Catholic University of Puerto
  Rico
School of Law
Avenida Las Americas Station 6
Ponce, PR 00732
809-841-2000

University of Chicago
Law School
1111 East 60th Street
Chicago, IL 60637
312-702-9494

University of Cincinnati
College of Law
P.O. Box 210040
Cincinnati, OH 45221
513-556-6805

Cleveland State University
Cleveland-Marshall College of
  Law
1801 Euclid Avenue
Cleveland, OH 44115
216-687-2304

University of Colorado
School of Law
Campus Box 403
Boulder, CO 80309
303-492-7203

Columbia University
School of Law
435 West 116th Street
New York, NY 10027
212-854-2670

University of Connecticut
School of Law
55 Elizabeth Street
Hartford, CT 06105
203-241-4696

Cornell Law School
Myron Taylor Hall
Ithaca, NY 14853
607-255-5141

Creighton University
School of Law
2500 California Street
Omaha, NE 68178
402-280-2872

University of Dayton
School of Law
300 College Park
Dayton, OH 45469-1320
513-229-3555

University of Denver
College of Law
7039 East 18th Street
Denver, CO 80220
303-871-6135

DePaul University
College of Law
25 East Jackson Boulevard
Chicago, IL 60604
312-362-6831

University of Detroit
School of Law
651 East Jefferson Avenue
Detroit, MI 48226
313-596-9848

Detroit College of Law
10210 North Business Complex
East Lansing, MI 48824
517-432-0222

Dickinson School of Law
150 South College Street
Carlisle, PA 17013
717-240-5207

District of Columbia
School of Law
719 13th Street, N.W.
Washington, DC 20005
202-274-7341

Drake University
Law School
2507 University Avenue
Des Moines, IA 50311
515-271-2782

Duke University
School of Law
Science and Riverview Drives
Box 90393
Durham, NC 27708
919-613-7020

Duquesne University
School of Law
900 Locust Street
Pittsburgh, PA 15282
412-398-6296

Emory University
School of Law
Gambrell Hall
Atlanta, GA 30322
404-727-6801

University of Florida
College of Law
325 Holland Hall
P.O. Box 117622
Gainesville, FL 32611
904-392-2087

Florida State University
College of Law
425 West Jefferson Street
Tallahassee, FL 32306
904-644-3787

Fordham University
School of Law
140 West 62nd Street
New York, NY 10023
212-626-6810

Franklin Pierce Law Center
2 White Street
Concord, NH 03301
603-228-9217

George Mason University
School of Law
3401 North Fairfax Drive
Arlington, VA 22201
703-993-8010

George Washington University
National Law Center
720 20th Street, N.W
Washington, DC 20052
202-994-7230

Georgetown University
Law Center
600 New Jersey Avenue, N.W.
Washington, DC 20001
202-662-9010

University of Georgia
School of Law
Athens, GA 30602
706-542-7060

Georgia State University
College of Law
P.O. Box 4037
Atlanta, GA 30302
404-651-2048

Golden Gate University
School of Law
536 Mission Street
San Francisco, CA 94105
415-442-6630

Gonzaga University
School of Law
Box 3528
Spokane, WA 99220
509-328-4220

Hamline University
School of Law
1536 Hewitt Avenue
St. Paul, MN 55104
612-641-2461

Harvard Law School
Cambridge, MA 02138
617-495-3109

University of Hawaii
William S. Richardson
School of Law
2515 Dole Street
Honolulu, HI 96822
808-956-3000

Hofstra University
School of Law
121 Hofstra University
Hempstead, NY 11550
516-463-5916

University of Houston
Law Center
Houston, TX 77204
713-743-1070

Howard University
School of Law
2900 Van Ness Street, N.W.
Washington, DC 20008
202-806-8008

University of Idaho
College of Law
6th and Rayburn
Moscow, ID 83844
208-885-6422

University of Illinois
College of Law
504 East Pennsylvania
Champaign, IL 61820
217-244-6415

Illinois Institute of Technology
Chicago-Kent College of Law
565 West Adams Street
Chicago, IL 60661
312-906-5020

Indiana University—
   Bloomington
School of Law
Law Building Room 230
Bloomington, IN 47405
812-855-2704

Indiana University—Indianapolis
School of Law
735 West New York Street
Indianapolis, IN 46202
317-274-2459

Inter American University of
   Puerto Rico
School of Law
P.O. Box 70351
San Juan, PR 00936
809-751-1912 ext. 2013

University of Iowa
College of Law
276 Boyd Law Building
Iowa City, IA 52242
319-335-9095

John Marshall Law School
315 South Plymouth Court
Chicago, IL 60604
312-987-1406

University of Kansas
School of Law
205 Green Hall
Lawrence, KS 66045
913-864-4378

University of Kentucky
College of Law
209 Law Building
Lexington, KY 40506-0048
606-257-7938

Lewis and Clark College
Northwestern School of Law
10015 Terwilliger Boulevard
Portland, OR 97219
503-768-6616

Louisiana State University
Paul M. Hebert Law Center
Baton Rouge, LA 70803
504-388-8646

University of Louisville
School of Law
2301 South 3rd Street
Louisville, KY 40292
502-588-6364

Loyola Law School
919 South Albany Street
Los Angeles, CA 90015
213-736-1180

Loyola University—Chicago
School of Law
One East Pearson Street
Chicago, IL 60611
312-915-7170

Loyola University—New Orleans
School of Law
7214 St. Charles Avenue
New Orleans, LA 70118
504-861-5575

University of Maine
School of Law
246 Deering Avenue
Portland, ME 04102

Marquette University
Law School
P.O. Box 1881
Milwaukee, WI 53201
414-288-6767

University of Maryland
School of Law
500 West Baltimore Street
Baltimore, MD 21201
410-706-3492

McGeorge School of Law
University of the Pacific
3200 Fifth Avenue
Sacramento, CA 95817
916-739-7105

University of Memphis
Humphreys School of Law
3715 Central Avenue
Memphis, TN 38152
901-678-2073

Mercer University
Walter F. George School of Law
1021 Georgia Avenue
Macon, GA 31201-6709
912-752-2605

University of Miami
School of Law
P.O. Box 248087
Coral Gables, FL 33124-8087
305-284-2523

University of Michigan
Law School
625 South State Street
Ann Arbor, MI 48109-1215
313-764-0537

University of Minnesota
Law School
229 19th Avenue South
Minneapolis, MN 55455
612-625-5005

University of Mississippi
School of Law
Lamar Hall
University, MS 38677
601-232-7361

Mississippi College
School of Law
151 East Griffith Street
Jackson, MS 39201
601-353-3907

University of Missouri—
   Columbia
School of Law
103 Holsten Hall
Columbia, MO 65211
314-882-6042

University of Missouri—Kansas
   City
School of Law
500 East 52nd Street
Kansas City, MO 64110
816-235-1644

University of Montana
School of Law
Missoula, MT 59812
406-243-2698

University of Nebraska
College of Law
40th and Holdrege
Lincoln, NE 68583-0902
402-472-2161

New England School of Law
154 Stuart Street
Boston, MA 02116
617-451-0010

University of New Mexico
School of Law
1117 Stanford Drive, N.E.
Albuquerque, NM 87131
505-277-5072

CUNY Law School at Queens
   College
65-21 Main Street
Flushing, NY 11367

SUNY at Buffalo
School of Law
O'Brien Hall
Buffalo, NY 14260
716-645-2060

New York Law School
57 Worth Street
New York, NY 10013
212-431-2888

New York University
School of Law
110 West Theo Street
New York, NY 10012
212-998-6060

University of North Carolina
School of Law
CB 3380
Chapel Hill, NC 27599-3380
919-962-5109

North Carolina Central
   University
School of Law
15129 Alston Avenue
Durham, NC 27707
919-560-6333

University of North Dakota
School of Law
Box 9003
Grand Forks, ND 58202
701-777-2104

Northeastern University
School of Law
P.O. Box 728
Boston, MA 02117
617-373-2395

Northern Illinois University
College of Law
Swen Parson Hall
DeKalb, IL 60115
815-753-1420

Northern Kentucky University
Salmon P. Chase College of Law
Nunn Hall
Highland Heights, KY 41076
606-572-6976

Northwestern University
School of Law
357 East Chicago Avenue
Chicago, IL 60611
312-503-8465

Notre Dame Law School
P.O. Box 959
Notre Dame, IN 46556
219-631-6626

Nova University
Shepard Broad Law Center
3105 College Avenue
Fort Lauderdale, FL 33314
954-452-6117

Ohio Northern University
Pettit College of Law
572 South Main Street
Ada, OH 45810
419-772-2211

Ohio State University
College of Law
55 West 12th Avenue
Drinko Hall
Columbus, OH 43210
614-292-8810

University of Oklahoma
College of Law
300 Timberdell Road
Norman, OK 73019
405-325-4726

Oklahoma City University
Law School
2501 North Blackwelder
Oklahoma City, OK 73106
405-521-5354

University of Oregon
School of Law
1221 University of Oregon
Eugene, OR 97403
541-346-3846

Pace University
School of Law
78 North Broadway
White Plains, NY 10603
914-422-4210

University of Pennsylvania
Law School
3400 Chestnut Street
Philadelphia, PA 19104
215-893-7400

Pepperdine University
School of Law
24255 Pacific Coast Highway
Malibu, CA 90263
310-456-4631

University of Pittsburgh
School of Law
3900 Forbes Avenue
Pittsburgh, PA 15260
412-648-1412

University of Puerto Rico
School of Law
P.O. Box 23349 UPR Station
Rio Pedras, PR 00931
809-764-1655

Quinnipiac College
School of Law
275 Mt. Carmel Avenue
Hamden, CT 06518
203-287-3400

Regent University School of Law
College of Law and Government
1000 Regent University Drive
Virginia Beach, VA 23464
804-597-4584

University of Richmond
School of Law
Richmond, VA 23173
804-289-8189

Rogers Williams University
School of Law
10 Metacon Drive
Bristol, RI 02809
401-254-4555

Rutgers University—Camden
School of Law
5th and Penn Streets
Camden, NJ 08102
609-757-6102

Rutgers University—Newark
School of Law
15 Washington Street
Newark, NJ 07102
201-648-5557

St. John's University
School of Law
800 West Utopia Parkway
Jamaica, NY 11439
718-990-6611

St. Louis University
School of Law
3700 Lindell Boulevard
St. Louis, MO 63108
314-977-2800

St. Mary's University of San
   Antonio
School of Law
One Camino Santa Maria
San Antonio, TX 78228
210-436-3523

St. Thomas University
School of Law
16400 N.W. 32nd Avenue
Miami, FL 33054
305-623-2310

Cumberland School of Law
Samford University
800 Lakeshore Drive
Birmingham, AL 35229
205-870-2702

University of San Diego
School of Law
5998 Alcala Park
San Diego, CA 92110
619-260-4528

University of San Francisco
School of Law
2130 Fulton Street
San Francisco, CA 94117-1080
415-666-6586

Santa Clara University
School of Law
Santa Clara, CA 95053
408-554-4800

Seton Hall University
School of Law
One Newark Center
Newark, NJ 07102
201-642-8747

University of South Carolina
School of Law
Main and Green Streets
Columbia, SC 29208
803-777-6605

University of South Dakota
School of Law
414 East Clark Street
Vermillion, SD 57069
605-677-5443

South Texas College of Law
1303 San Jacinto
Houston, TX 77002
713-646-1810

University of Southern
  California
Law Center
University Park
Los Angeles, CA 90089-0071
213-740-7331

Southern Illinois University
School of Law
Lesar Law Building
Carbondale, IL 62901
618-453-8767

Southern Methodist University
School of Law
P.O. Box 750110
Dallas, TX 75275
214-768-2550

Southern University
Law Center
P.O. Box 9294
Baton Rouge, LA 70813
504-771-5340

Southwestern University
School of Law
675 South Westmoreland Avenue
Los Angeles, CA 90005-3992
213-738-6717

Stanford Law School
Crown Quadrangle
Stanford, CA 94305
415-723-4985

Stetson University
College of Law
1401 61st Street South
St. Petersburg, FL 33707
813-345-1121, ext. 214

Suffolk University
Law School
41 Temple Street
Boston, MA 02114
617-573-8144

Syracuse University
College of Law
Syracuse, NY 13244
315-443-1962

Temple University
School of Law
1719 North Broad Street
Philadelphia, PA 19122
215-204-8925

University of Tennessee
College of Law
104 Aconda Court
Knoxville, TN 37996
423-974-4131

University of Texas
School of Law
727 East 26th Street
Austin, TX 78705
512-471-8268

Texas Southern University
Thurgood Marshall School of
  Law
3100 Cleburne Avenue
Houston, TX 77004
713-313-7114

Texas Tech University
School of Law
1802 Hartford
Lubbock, TX 79409
806-742-3985

Texas Wesleyan University
School of Law
2535 Grauwyler Road East
Irving, TX 75061
214-579-5751

Thomas M. Cooley Law School
217 South Capitol Avenue
P.O. Box 13038
Lansing, MI 48901
517-371-5140

University of Toledo
College of Law
2801 West Bancroft Street
Toledo, OH 43606
419-530-4131

Touro College
Jacob D. Fuchsberg Law Center
300 Nassau Road
Huntington, NY 11743
516-421-2244

Tulane University
School of Law
Weinmann Hall
6329 Freret Street
New Orleans, LA 70118
504-865-5930

University of Tulsa
College of Law
3120 East Fourth Place
Tulsa, OK 74104
918-631-2709

University of Utah
College of Law
Salt Lake City, UT 84112
801-581-7479

Valparaiso University
School of Law
Wasemann Hall
Valparaiso, IN 46383
219-465-7829

Vanderbilt University
School of Law
Nashville, TN 37240
615-322-6452

Vermont Law School
P.O. Box 96
South Royalton, VT 05068
802-763-8303

Villanova University
School of Law
Garey Hall
Villanova, PA 19085
601-519-7010

University of Virginia
School of Law
580 Massie Road
Charlottesville, VA 22903
804-924-7351

Wake Forest University
School of Law
P.O. Box 7206, Reynolda Station
Winston-Salem, NC 27109
910-759-5437

Washburn University
School of Law
1700 College
Topeka, KS 66621
913-231-1185

University of Washington
School of Law
1100 N.E. Campus Parkway
Seattle, WA 98105
206-543-4078

Washington and Lee University
School of Law
Lewis Hall
Lexington, VA 24450
540-463-8504

Washington University
School of Law
One Brookings Drive
Campus Box 1120
St. Louis, MO 63130
314-935-4525

Wayne State University
Law School
468 West Ferry
Detroit, MI 48202
313-577-3937

West Virginia University
College of Law
P.O. Box 6130
Morgantown, WV 26506

Western New England College
School of Law
1215 Wilbraham Road
Springfield, MA 01119
413-782-1406

Whittier College
School of Law
5353 West Third Street
Los Angeles, CA 90020
213-938-3621 ext. 123

Widener University
School of Law
P.O. Box 7474, Concord Pike
Wilmington, DE 19803
302-477-2162

Willamette University
College of Law
900 State Street
Salem, OR 97301
503-370-6282

College of William and Mary
Marshall-Wythe School of Law
P.O. Box 8795
Williamsburg, VA 23185
804-221-3785

William Mitchell College of Law
875 Summit Avenue
St. Paul, MN 55105
612-290-6329

University of Wisconsin
Law School
975 Bascom Hall
Madison, WI 53706
608-262-5914

University of Wyoming
College of Law
University Station Box 3035
Laramie, WY 82071
307-766-6416

Yale Law School
P.O. Box 208329
New Haven, CT 06520
203-432-4995

U.S. LAW SCHOOLS NOT APPROVED BY THE AMERICAN BAR ASSOCIATION

American College of Law
1717 South State
   College Boulevard #100
Anaheim, CA 92806
714-643-3699

Atlanta Law School
880 West Peachtree Street, N.W.
Suite B
Atlanta, GA 30309

CAL Northern School of Law
2525 Dominic Drive
Chico, CA 95928

California Southern
   Law School
3775 Elizabeth Street
Riverside, CA 92506

Central California College
School of Law
925 "N" Street #110
Fresno, CA 93721

CLEO—Council on Legal
   Education Opportunity
1800 M Street, N.W.
Suite 290, North Lobby
Washington, DC 20036

Empire College
3033 Cleveland Avenue
Suite 102
Santa Rosa, CA 95403
707-546-4000

Florida Coastal School of Law
7555 Beach Boulevard
Jacksonville, FL 32216
904-724-6699

Glendale University
College of Law
220 North Glendale Avenue
Glendale, CA 91206
818-247-0700

Guild Law School
People's College of Law
660 South Bonnie Brea Street
Los Angeles, CA 90057
213-483-0083

Humphreys College of Law
6650 Inglewood Avenue
Stockton, CA 95207
209-478-0800

John Marshall Law School—
   Atlanta
805 Peachtree Street, N.E.
Suite 400
Atlanta, GA 30308
404-872-3593

John F. Kennedy University
School of Law
547 Ygnacio Valley Road
Walnut Creek, CA 94596
510-295-1800

Jones School of Law
5345 Atlanta Highway
Montgomery, AL 36109
205-260-6210

University of LaVerne
College of Law
1950 3rd Street
LaVerne, CA 91750
909-596-1848

Lincoln Law School of
  Sacramento
3140 J Street
Box 160328
Sacramento, CA 95816
916-446-1275

Nashville School of Law
2934 South Cleo Drive
Nashville, TN 37204
615-256-3684

New College of California
  Law School
50 Fell Street
San Francisco, CA 94102
415-241-1353

Pacific Coast University School
  of Law
440 Redondo Avenue
Long Beach, CA 90814

Peninsula University
College of Law
436 Dell Avenue
Mountain View, CA 94043
415-964-5044

San Francisco Law School
20 Haight Street
San Francisco, CA 94102
415-626-5550

Santa Barbara College of Law
911 Tremonto Road
Santa Barbara, CA 93103
805-569-1567

Simon Greenleaf School of Law
3855 East LaPalma Avenue
Anaheim, CA 92807

Southern New England School of
  Law
333 Faunce Corner Road
North Dartmouth, MA 02747
508-998-9400

Thomas Jefferson
  School of Law
2121 San Diego Avenue
San Diego, CA 92110
619-297-9700

Western Sierra Law School
8376 Hercules Street
La Mesa, CA 91942

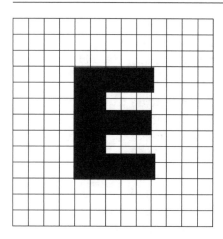

APPENDIX E:
MODEL RULES OF
PROFESSIONAL CONDUCT

PREAMBLE: A LAWYER'S RESPONSIBILITIES

A lawyer is a representative of clients, an officer of the legal system, and a public citizen having special responsibility for the quality of justice.

As a representative of clients, a lawyer performs various functions. As advisor, a lawyer provides a client with an informed understanding of the client's legal rights and obligations and explains their practical implications. As advocate, a lawyer zealously asserts the client's position under the rules of the adversary system. As negotiator, a lawyer seeks a result advantageous to the client but consistent with requirements of honest dealing with others. As intermediary between clients, a lawyer seeks to reconcile their divergent interests as an advisor and, to a limited extent, as a spokesperson for each client. A lawyer acts as evaluator by examining a client's legal affairs and reporting about them to the client or to others.

In all professional functions a lawyer should be competent, prompt, and diligent. A lawyer should maintain communication with a client concerning the representation. A lawyer should keep in confidence information relating to representation of a client except so far as disclosure is required or permitted by the Rules of Professional Conduct or other law.

A lawyer's conduct should conform to the requirements of the law, both in professional service to clients and in the lawyer's business and personal affairs. A lawyer should use the law's procedures only for legitimate purposes and not to harass or intimidate others. A lawyer should demonstrate respect for the legal system and for those who serve it, including judges, other lawyers and public officials. While it is a lawyer's duty, when necessary, to challenge the rectitude of official action, it is also a lawyer's duty to uphold legal process.

As a public citizen, a lawyer should seek improvement of the law, the administration of justice and the quality of service rendered by the legal profession. As a member of a learned profession, a lawyer should cultivate knowledge of the law beyond its use for clients, employ that knowledge in reform of the law, and work to strengthen legal education. A lawyer should be mindful of deficiencies in the administration of justice and of the fact that the poor, and sometimes persons who are not poor, cannot afford adequate legal assistance, and should therefore devote professional time and civic influence in their behalf. A lawyer should aid the legal profession in pursuing these objectives and should help the bar regulate itself in the public interest.

Many of a lawyer's professional responsibilities are prescribed in the Rules of Professional Conduct, as well as substantive and procedural law. However, a lawyer is also guided by personal conscience and the approbation of professional peers. A lawyer should strive to attain the highest level of skill, to improve the law and the legal profession and to exemplify the legal profession's ideals of public service.

A lawyer's responsibilities as a representative of clients, an officer of the legal system, and a public citizen are usually harmonious. Thus, when an opposing party is well represented, a lawyer can be a zealous advocate on behalf of a client and at the same time assume that justice is being done. So also, a lawyer can be sure that preserving client confidences ordinarily serves the public interest because people are more likely to seek legal advice, and thereby heed their legal obligations, when they know their communications will be private.

In the nature of law practice, however, conflicting responsibilities are encountered. Virtually all difficult ethical problems arise from conflict between a lawyer's responsibilities to clients, to the legal system and to the lawyer's own interest in remaining an upright person while earning a satisfactory living. The Rules of Professional Conduct prescribe terms for resolving such conflicts. Within the framework of these Rules many difficult issues of professional discretion can arise. Such issues must be resolved through the exercise of sensitive professional and moral judgment guided by the basic principles underlying the Rules.

The legal profession is largely self-governing. Although other professions also have been granted powers of self-government, the legal profession is unique in this respect because of the close relationship between the profession and the processes of government and law enforcement. This connection is manifested in the fact that ultimate authority over the legal profession is vested largely in the courts.

To the extent that lawyers meet the obligations of their professional calling, the occasion for government regulation is obviated. Self-regulation also helps maintain the legal profession's independence from government domination. An independent legal profession is an important force in preserving government under law, for abuse of legal authority is more readily challenged by a profession whose members are not dependent on government for the right to practice.

The legal profession's relative autonomy carries with it special responsibilities of self-government. The profession has a responsibility to assure that its regulations are conceived in the public interest and not in furtherance of parochial or self-interested concerns of the bar. Every lawyer is responsible for observance of the Rules of Professional Conduct. A lawyer should also aid in securing their observance by other lawyers. Neglect of these responsibilities compromises the independence of the profession and the public interest which it serves. Lawyers play a vital role in the preservation of society. The fulfillment of the role requires an understanding by lawyers of their relationship to our legal system. The Rules of Professional Conduct, when properly applied, serve to define that relationship.

RULE 1.1 Competence

A lawyer shall provide competent representation to a client. Competent representation requires the legal knowledge, skill, thoroughness and preparation reasonably necessary for the representation.

RULE 1.2 Scope of Representation

(a) A lawyer shall abide by a client's decisions concerning the objectives of representation, subject to paragraphs (c), (d) and (e), and shall consult with the client as to the means by which they are to be pursued. A lawyer shall abide by a client's decision whether to accept an offer of settlement of a matter. In a criminal case, the lawyer shall abide by the client's decision, after consultation with the lawyer, as to a plea to be entered, whether to waive jury trial and whether the client will testify.

(b) A lawyer's representation of a client, including representation by appointment, does not constitute an endorsement of the client's political, economic, social or moral views or activities.

(c) A lawyer may limit the objectives of the representation if the client consents after consultation.

(d) A lawyer shall not counsel a client to engage, or assist a client, in conduct that the lawyer knows is criminal or fraudulent, but a lawyer may discuss the legal consequences of any proposed course of conduct with a client and may counsel or assist a client to make a good faith effort to determine the validity, scope, meaning, or application of the law.

(e) When a lawyer knows that a client expects assistance not permitted by the Rules of Professional Conduct or other law, the lawyer shall consult with the client regarding the relevant limitations on the lawyer's conduct.

RULE 1.3 Diligence

A lawyer shall act with reasonable diligence and promptness in representing a client.

RULE 1.4 Communication

(a) A lawyer shall keep a client reasonably informed about the status of a matter and promptly comply with reasonable requests for information.

(b) A lawyer shall explain a matter to the extent reasonably necessary to permit the client to make informed decisions regarding the representation.

RULE 2.1 Advisor

In representing a client, a lawyer shall exercise independent professional judgment and render candid advice. In rendering advice, a lawyer may refer not only to law but to other considerations such as moral, economic, social and political factors, that may be relevant to the client's situation.

RULE 2.2 Intermediary

(a) A lawyer may act as intermediary between clients if:

(1) the lawyer consults with each client concerning the implications of the common representation, including the advantages and risks involved, and the effect on the attorney-client privileges, and obtains each client's consent to the common representation;

(2) the lawyer reasonably believes that the matter can be resolved on terms compatible with the clients' best interests, that each client will be able to make adequately informed decisions in the matter and that there is little risk of material prejudice to the interest of any of the clients if the contemplated resolution is unsuccessful; and

(3) the lawyer reasonably believes that the common representation can be undertaken impartially and without improper effect on other responsibilities the lawyer has to any of the clients.

(b) While acting as intermediary, the lawyer shall consult with each client concerning the decisions to be made and the considerations relevant in making them, so that each client can make adequately informed decisions.

(c) A lawyer shall withdraw as intermediary if any of the clients so request, or if any of the conditions stated in paragraph (a) is no longer satisfied. Upon withdrawal, the lawyer shall not continue to represent any of the clients in the matter that was the subject of the intermediation.

RULE 2.3 Evaluation for Use by Third Persons

(a) A lawyer may undertake an evaluation of a matter affecting a client for the use of someone other than the client if:

(1) the lawyer reasonably believes that making the evaluation is compatible with other aspects of the lawyer's relationship with the client; and

(2) the client consents after consultation.

(b) Except as disclosure is required in connection with a report of an evaluation, information relating to the evaluation is otherwise protected by rule 1.6.

RULE 3.1 Meritorious Claims and Contentions

A lawyer shall not bring or defend a proceeding, or assert or controvert an issue therein, unless there is a basis for doing so that is not frivolous, which includes a good faith argument for an extension, modification, or reversal of existing law. A lawyer for the defendant in a criminal proceeding, or the respondent in a proceeding that could result in incarceration, may nevertheless so defend the proceeding as to require that every element of the case be established.

RULE 3.2 Expediting Litigation

A lawyer shall make reasonable efforts to expedite litigation consistent with the interests of the client.

RULE 1.15 Safekeeping Property

(a) A lawyer shall hold property of clients or third persons that is in a lawyer's possession in connection with a representation separate from the lawyer's own property. Funds shall be kept in a separate account maintained in the state where the lawyer's office is situated, or elsewhere with the consent of the client or third person. Other property shall be identified as such and appropriately safeguarded. Complete records of such account funds and other property shall be kept by the lawyer and shall be preserved for a period of [five years] after termination of the representation.

(b) Upon receiving funds or other property in which a client or third person has an interest, a lawyer shall promptly notify the client or third person. Except as stated in this rule or otherwise permitted by law or by agreement with the client, a lawyer shall promptly deliver to the client or third person any funds or other property that the client or third person is entitled to receive and, upon request by the client or third person, shall promptly render a full accounting regarding such property.

(c) When in the course of representation a lawyer is in possession of property in which both the lawyer and another person claim interests, the property shall be kept separate by the lawyer until there is an accounting and severance of their interest. If a dispute arises concerning their respective interests, the portion in dispute shall be kept separate by the lawyer until the dispute is resolved.

RULE 5.1 Responsibilities of a Partner or Supervisory Lawyer

(a) A partner in a law firm shall make reasonable efforts to ensure that the firm has in effect measures giving reasonable assurance that all lawyers in the firm conform to the rules of professional conduct.

(b) A lawyer having direct supervisory authority over another lawyer shall make reasonable efforts to ensure that the other lawyer conforms to the rules of professional conduct.

(c) A lawyer shall be responsible for another lawyer's violation of the rules of professional conduct if:

(1) the lawyer orders or, with knowledge of the specific conduct, ratifies the conduct involved; or

(2) the lawyer is a partner in the law firm in which the other lawyer practices, or has direct supervisory authority over the other lawyer, and knows of the conduct at a time when its consequences can be avoided or mitigated but fails to take reasonable remedial action.

RULE 5.2 Responsibilities of a Subordinate Lawyer

(a) A lawyer is bound by the rules of professional conduct notwithstanding that the lawyer acted at the direction of another person.

(b) A Subordinate lawyer does not violate the rules of professional conduct if that lawyer acts in accordance with a supervisory lawyer's reasonable resolution of an arguable question of professional duty.

RULE 5.3 Responsibilities Regarding Nonlawyer Assistants

With respect to a nonlawyer employed or retained by or associated with a lawyer:

(a) a partner in a law firm shall make reasonable efforts to ensure that the firm has in effect measures giving reasonable assurance that the person's conduct is compatible with the professional obligations of the lawyer;

(b) a lawyer having direct supervisory authority over the nonlawyer shall make reasonable efforts to ensure that the person's conduct is compatible with the professional obligations of the lawyer; and

(c) a lawyer shall be responsible for conduct of such a person that would be a violation of the rules of professional conduct if engaged in by a lawyer if:

(1) the lawyer orders or, with the knowledge of the specific conduct, ratifies the conduct involved; or

(2) the lawyer is a partner in the law firm in which the person is employed, or has direct supervisory authority over the person, and knows of the conduct at a time when its consequences can be avoided or mitigated but fails to take reasonable remedial action.

RULE 5.4 Professional Independence of a Lawyer

(a) A lawyer or law firm shall not share legal fees with a nonlawyer, except that:

(1) an agreement by a lawyer with the lawyer's firm, partner, or associate may provide for the payment of money, over a reasonable period of time after the lawyer's death, to the lawyer's estate or to one or more specified persons;

(2) a lawyer who undertakes to complete unfinished legal business of a deceased lawyer may pay to the estate of the deceased lawyer that proportion of the total compensation which fairly represents the services rendered by the deceased lawyer; and

(3) a lawyer or law firm may include nonlawyer employees in a compensation or retirement plan, even though the plan is based in whole or in part on a profit-sharing arrangement.

(b) A lawyer shall not form a partnership with a nonlawyer if any of the activities of the partnership consist of the practice of law.

(c) A lawyer shall not permit a person who recommends, employs, or pays the lawyer to render legal services for another to direct or regulate the lawyer's professional judgment in rendering such legal services.

(d) A lawyer shall not practice with or in the form of a professional corporation or association authorized to practice law for a profit, if:

(1) a nonlawyer owns any interest therein, except that a fiduciary representative of the estate of a lawyer may hold the stock or interest of the lawyer for a reasonable time during administration:

(2) a nonlawyer is a corporate director or officer thereof; or

(3) a nonlawyer has the right to direct or control the professional judgment of a lawyer.

RULE 5.5 Unauthorized Practice of Law

A lawyer shall not:

(a) practice law in a jurisdiction where doing so violates the regulations of the legal profession in that jurisdiction; or

(b) assist a person who is not a member of the bar in the performance of activity that constitutes the unauthorized practice of law.

RULE 7.1 Communications Concerning a Lawyer's Services

A lawyer shall not make a false or misleading communication about the lawyer or the lawyer's services. A communication is false or misleading if it:

(a) contains a material misrepresentation of fact or law, or omits a fact necessary to make the statement considered as a whole not materially misleading;

(b) is likely to create an unjustified expectation about results the lawyer can achieve, or states or implies that the lawyer can achieve results by means that violate the rules of professional conduct or other law; or

(c) compares the lawyer's services with other lawyers' services, unless the comparison can be factually substantiated.

RULE 8.1 Bar Admission and Disciplinary Matters

An applicant for admission to the bar, or a lawyer in connection with a bar admission application or in connection with a disciplinary matter, shall not:

(a) knowingly make a false statement of material facts; or

(b) fail to disclose a fact necessary to correct a misapprehension known by the person to have arisen in the matter, or knowingly fail to respond to a lawful demand for information from an admission or disciplinary authority, except that this rule does not require disclosure of information otherwise protected by rule 1.6.

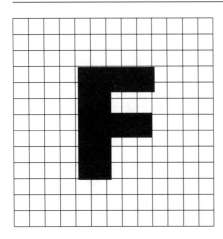

APPENDIX F: BIBLIOGRAPHY

This bibliography represents a very short sampling of books about law, lawyers, and legal careers. All the titles were selected because they have something specific to say to the college student embarking upon a legal education. The selections generally include books published since 1980, although a few earlier works of lasting value are mentioned as well.

Most of these books can be obtained through a library or commercial bookstore. Those readers who have been intrigued by the possibility of a career in law undoubtedly will want to read more. In addition to the books mentioned here, several periodicals publish excellent articles about the legal profession on a fairly regular basis. These include: *The American Lawyer, The National Law Journal, The American Bar Association Journal, Student Lawyer, Lawyer's Alert,* and *The New York Times.*

1995 Employment Report and Salary Survey. Washington, DC: National Association for Law Placement, 1996.

Arron, Deborah and Deborah Guyol. *The Complete Guide to Contract Lawyering.* Seattle, WA: Niche Press, 1995.

———. *Running from the Law: Why Good Lawyers Are Getting Out of the Law.* Seattle, WA: Niche Press, 1989.

———. *What Can You Do With a Law Degree?* Seattle, WA: Niche Press, 1992.

Bay, Monica. *Careers in Civil Litigation.* Chicago: American Bar Association, 1990.

Bell, Susan J., ed. *Full Disclosure: Do You Really Want to Be a Lawyer?* Princeton, NJ: Peterson's, 1989.

Bolles, Richard N. *The Three Boxes of Life and How to Get Out of Them.* Berkeley, CA: Ten Speed Press, 1987.

Bolles, Richard N. *What Color Is Your Parachute?* Berkeley, CA: Ten Speed Press, 1991.

Cooper, Cynthia. *The Insider's Guide to the Top Fifteen Law Schools.* New York: Doubleday, 1990.

Couric, Emily. *Women Lawyers: Perspectives on Success.* New York: HBJ Law and Business, 1984.

Curran, Barbara and Clara N. Carson. *The Lawyers Statistical Report: The U.S. Legal Profession in the 1990s.* Chicago: American Bar Foundation, 1994.

Fox, Ronald W. *Law Pursuit: Careers in Public Interest Law.* Chicago, IL: American Bar Association, 1992.

Green, Jonathan Clark, ed. *ILSA Guide to Educational and Career Development in International Law.* Washington, DC: American Society of International Law, 1991.

Guide to Small Firm Employment. Washington, DC: National Association for Law Placement, 1992.

Jaszaczal, Sandra, ed. *Encyclopedia of Associations,* 26th edition. Detroit: Gale Research, Co., 1996.

Killoughey, Donna M., ed. *Breaking Traditions: Work Alternatives for Lawyers.* Chicago, IL: American Bar Association, 1993.

Maer, Janis, ed. *Careers in International Law.* Chicago, IL: American Bar Association, 1993.

Malkani, Sheila V. and Michael F. Walsh. *Insider's Guide to Law Firms.* Boulder, CO: Mobius Press, 1994.

Mantis, Hillary Jane and Kathleen Brady. *Jobs for Lawyers: Effective Techniques for Getting Hired in Today's Legal Marketplace.* Manassas, VA: Impact Publications, 1996.

McNeil, Heidi L. *Changing Jobs: A Handbook for the 1990s.* Chicago, IL: American Bar Association, 1994.

Munneke, Gary A. *Barron's Guide to Law Schools,* 12th edition. Hauppauge, NY: Barron's, 1996.

———. *How to Succeed in Law School.* Hauppauge, NY: Barron's 1993.

———. *The Legal Career Guide: From Law Student to Lawyer.* Chicago: American Bar Association, 1992.

———. *Materials and Cases on Law Practice Management.* St. Paul, MN: West, 1991.

——— and William D. Henslee. *Non-Legal Careers for Lawyers.* Chicago: American Bar Association, 1993.

———. *Opportunities in Law Careers.* Lincolnwood, IL: VGM Career Horizons, 1994.

Robinson, David A. *Practicing Law Without Clients: Making a Living as a Freelance Lawyer.* Chicago, IL: American Bar Association, 1996.

Scheele, Adele. *Skills for Success.* New York: Ballantine Books, 1981.

Sheehy, Gail. *Passages.* New York: Ballantine Books, 1977.

Shropshire, Kenneth L. *Careers in Sports Law.* Chicago: American Bar Association, 1990.

Stevens, Marc. *Power of Attorney: The Rise and Fall of the Great Law Firms.* New York: McGraw-Hill, 1987.

Stewart, James B. *The Partners: America's Most Powerful Law Firms.* New York: Simon & Schuster, 1983.

Turow, Scott. *One L.* New York: Putnam, 1977.

Vogt, Leona M. *From Law School to Career: Where Do Graduates Go and What Do They Do?* Cambridge, MA: Harvard Law School, 1986.

Zemans, Frances Kahn and Victor Rosenblum. *The Making of a Public Profession.* Chicago: American Bar Foundation, 1981.